Live
Out
Loud

FOLLOWING YOUR PURPOSE EVEN WHEN IT'S HARD

Moe Nicole

Published by Live out Loud Press

Edited by: Angee Costa & Moe Nicole

Book Cover by: Emmanuel Olamiriki

Library of Congress number: 2019914286

ISBN-13: *Paperback*

978-1-7340606-1-4

Table of Contents

PAGE 5
Introduction

PAGE 13
Chapter 1: When it's time to live OUT LOUD

PAGE 24
Chapter 2: When it's purpose-driven

PAGE 37
Chapter 3: When it's already yours

PAGE 52
Chapter 4: When you're finding your purpose

PAGE 63
Chapter 5: When you find your village

PAGE 78
Chapter 6: When it is hard

PAGE 91
Chapter 7: When it's meant for your harm

PAGE 102
Chapter 8: When boundaries are needed

PAGE 114
Chapter 9: When you find peace in failure

3

"The journey to your purpose is not easy, but it is worthwhile."

Rest in Love, Granny B.

Live out loud

Introduction

During the Fall of 2012, I visited Kenya, Africa for a couple weeks on a mission trip. During our time there, we worked with community members within their schools, medical missions, and community volunteer efforts. Before going, I had so many people filling my head up with what I would "see" when I got there. They would make comments such as:

"Oh my goodness that's so nice of you to go over there and help them people."
"I couldn't imagine living the way they have to live."
"Those poor people."

You get my drift on where those comments were going, right? *insert eye roll*

Honestly, those were the least passive ones I heard. We have all seen at least one commercial on TV exploiting "poor" children in Africa, guilt tripping you to send a donation to help them. We are shown a glimpse of what may be the reality of some people on the continent, but never the whole picture. To be honest, I didn't know what I was getting into either as we prepared to embark on the journey. I just knew it couldn't be as bad as the picture society had been painting for us.

And it wasn't.

What I saw when I got there was nowhere near what we see on TV. Yes, we saw people who lived in different conditions than what we may be used to. But no one... and I mean NO ONE was without joy. Despite their current circumstances, they had joy in their hearts. They were living out loud within their personal lives and making the best of their different situations. As I began to travel more, I found the same thing in Cuba and Ghana as well. Each one of these places helped enrich me mentally and emotionally as it pushed me to begin looking at life from a different lens. Cuba and Ghana were both a reminder of the lessons Kenya taught me, more specifically, about appreciating the simple things in life.

Upon my return from Kenya my shopping habits changed. I literally went into my closet and started getting rid of items I didn't need. I had seen a whole community of people with far less than me materially who were the most joyous and happy people despite what they were *lacking*. It was my trip to visit the elders where I realized they were wealthier than most people I knew. When we think of wealth, we have been taught to view it as how much money we have.

But it's so much more than that.

Wealth is joy and richness of life, love, and peace. You can be the richest person in the world yet be the most unfulfilled. Money is not the teacher of life: The teacher is the peace you have in your heart when you're staring into the dark ceiling. The instruction that peace gives is abundant and provides everlasting joy.

I saw this peace in a group of elders in Kenya. We visited a Kikuyu village community center that was for the elderly. Elders ranging from 60 to 102 years old walked to this center, as a way to fellowship with each other, once a week.

At the center we ate porridge served from a large pan, danced, sang to drums, and talked. I will be honest and say, as much as I enjoyed our elders, I didn't like the porridge the same. It tasted like cream of wheat, and I hate cream of wheat. Once we finished eating and settled down, they performed a naming ceremony. One of the elders, Maria, gave me the name of Waithira. Waithira is the name of one of Gikuyu's princesses who later married and created one of the nine tribes. Waithira is said to be born during the rainy season, loved music, and had vivid dreams. What interested me so much was that all these characteristics related to me.

I was forever inspired.

I adopted Maria as my godmother, and she will forever have a place in my heart. Her wisdom and intuition made a mark on my soul within only a couple hours of my life. She had joy. She was living out loud, just like most of the other elders at the center. They were proud of who they were, where they were from, and each other. That was all that mattered to them.

They are a great example of the fact that anyone is able to live out loud. It is not exclusive to the young single person enjoying life; it includes our elders too. There is no set time to start living out loud. Our elders bring so much joy and understanding of life when they accept who they are and know their purpose. My grandmother used to always say, before passing, "I'm 82 years old, I'm not going to live forever." I didn't accept that, I thought she was just saying something to ease my fears, by reminding me that death is a natural process of life.

But, she knew. She knew who she was, she knew her purpose, and she was okay with living in the moment. She was ok with what was to come, because she gave her energy to what was. That is where she found her joy.

That is where we each find our joy.

That's my challenge in this book, that we find our joy in the now, enjoy our personal journeys, and keep moving towards our purpose and goals. Not only do I want us all to live in our personal journeys, I want us to feel our purpose within it. That is my challenge as you continue to read.

Little girls are often raised with the thought of wanting to be a princess, floating across the ceramic floor in high heels, playing with wigs, tea sets, and lip gloss. We may even use baby dolls to teach us to embrace our nurturing side. Despite how cute this was, how did it feel for the little girl who didn't really like those things? What about the girl who likes to climb trees, play fight with neighborhood kids, explore, and read chapter books? She's often an outsider. She may feel like me. Heck, who am I kidding? She was me.

As a little girl, most times I felt timid, defensive, and alone. I never felt like I fit in with the masses in any of the environments I found myself in. In those quiet moments alone, I'd read from my favorite books, write short stories, and poems as I thought about life from a different perspective. These were all an escape from a world that left me feeling like being different was wrong. I didn't want to be wrong; I wanted to feel heard even in my silence. I wanted to feel welcomed in my environments. Many of us have experienced the feeling of being lonely, even in a room full of people. What is more tragic than an empty soul in a sea of fish?

The feeling of being lonely in itself is not a peaceful one; but being lonely while you're around other people is isolating. It creates the urge for fight or flight and a constant feeling of being on the defense. But from what? What about it makes us feel lonely? What about being in the crowd makes us feel invisible? Honestly, I don't think it has to do with the other people, more than it has to do with ourselves. There's a reason why we feel misunderstood, silenced, and unheard. That reason is our purpose and our connection with it.

Life teaches us to suppress a large part of ourselves, in an attempt to fit into society and our family's view of professionalism, what we should do or look like, what our purpose in life is, and how we get there. It's like society has created somewhat of a utopian opinion of what is right and wrong. Here's a fun fact: Society is WRONG! Growing up in this box has forced so many of us to preserve and suppress our true feelings, passions, and purpose in order to do what society tells us is the right thing. In turn, we suffer internally.

We live in an environment that tells you that it is not smart to quit a good paying career job to go back to school. We live in a society that tells you that you should only have *natural colored* hair in the workplace (yes, I've had this happen...). We live in a society that tells you it's not smart to get tattoos or piercings because it makes you less hirable. We live in a society that tells you there is a set of procedures and rules that are required for you to follow in order to find your happy place. We live in a society that makes it hard for people who are different.

I'm here to tell you now, this is not and does not have to be your truth if you don't want it to be. What your parents, siblings, friends, and spouse is telling you may not be your actual path or truth. That's why it's important for us to remain rooted, so we know when something is for us or not.

I am a witness.

Those who have been following me for a while are familiar with my favorite hashtag: #liveoutloud. I honestly put it on everything that represents me, or anything about living in truth, because it perfectly conveys my truth. But, I've never actually stated WHY I love the hashtag; it has always had a secret meaning to me. Some people have joined the movement and have added the hashtag as a comment here and there, and kept it moving. In my head, I'm saying to myself, "oh yea, they get it!" Living out loud is encouraging and motivating.

I started using the hashtag around the time I began the process of publishing my second book, They Never Told. They Never Told is a book that discusses unreported childhood sexual assault from the viewpoint of four adult survivors. The main premise of the book was the brutal honesty that our children are afraid to speak their truths, especially to adults. As I wrote the different experiences of the people, one being myself, I was reminded that this was when I began speaking my truth—when I began to feel free.

In my head, it was not only time to put an end to childhood sexual assault, but also to children not feeling safe and comfortable enough to speak their personal truths. I wrote the book as a way to speak out, and I wanted to create a movement of people who saw the benefit and meaning behind living out loud in our truths rather than continuing in silence and fear. There are so many people, couples, and families living in silence and untruth. These untruths are tearing us apart when what we need most is healing.

Chapter 1

When it's time to live OUT LOUD!

Since you have gotten through the introduction, you may be asking yourself, "OK, so what exactly does it mean to live out loud?" I gave a quick overview of where the term/hashtag #LiveOutLoud came from, but now it's time to get a little deeper. I'm going to break it down a little bit, because I want to make sure that when you're done reading this book, you will be able to go and live aloud in your personal truths and journey.

So let's start with the first word: live. The term "live" is defined as "to have life and be capable." What that means is, for you to live, you must be capable of having life within you. Life is the being of all things breathing, living, and growing. It is always changing, developing, and morphing into another phase of being.

Now, let's look at the second word: out. This one is simpler in context. "Out" basically means something that is not hidden inside; it is exposed. It isn't hidden, and it can be identified and found. One time we may hear the word "out" is when someone or something is exposed in some way.

Ex: Mary outed Sam on social media for cheating on his wife. She outed him by sharing screenshots of him from her social media messages, also known as 'DMs'.

In this example, the term "out" basically means being put into the public arena or in the eyes/direction of others in a way to gain attention. I think you get my point now when it comes to the word "out" and its relationship to living out loud. We are capable of being open about life and our experiences. This leads us to the last piece: LOUD! The funny thing about this one is that so many people used to make fun of me and try to make me feel bad for being so loud. The reality is, I just can't help it: LIKE REALLY! I talk loud. *I'm shrugging as I type this.*

The word "loud" speaks for itself and it is the most important piece to the phrase. To be loud you must carry sound, which is the opposite of silence. With that being said, to Live out Loud is to live within your personal truths and not be afraid of outing those things that may not "look good." It is also a time for us to basically live our best life simply because it is ours. In order to live out loud, we must be comfortable with our personal circumstances, goals, purposes, and visions. We must be in-tune with ourselves.

Check in: Have you ever found yourself doubting yourself in response to your current personal circumstances? How did you handle it? Did you

14

keep it to yourself, did you tell trusted friends, or did you blast it to the world?

_____

_____

_____

_____

_____

_____

_____

_____

_____

_____

Alright, let's bring it back now? What were your answers to the questions at the check-in? It's ok to be honest with yourself as you think about it. I'm going to share a little bit about myself because I know it can be hard when we only know our personal answers.

Most of my adulthood, I've heard people telling me how much they admire my personality and drive. From the outside looking in, it looked like I have always been living my best life.

Confession: I spent a nice amount of my life living from a really insecure place. I'd constantly look at where I was personally regretting past decisions, and wishing to live a totally different life. Although, on the other side of the fence, there were people wishing they could have the life I was living. I didn't see that; I only saw what I was living through at the moment. Not only was I living through the brink of depression, I was experiencing it alone—in silence. I didn't feel comfortable talking to people around me about it because I feared severe judgement. I was so far into my insecurities, that I was suicidal in high school. I am not ashamed of this because it is my truth. Because of this truth, I will always have my semi-colon tattoo to remind myself of where I have grown from.

We hear people scrutinize others so much that it can make us afraid to be vulnerable with the very people we should be able to trust with our deepest feelings. That was not my case. For a long time, I hated it, and no one else knew but me. To me, this was an unsafe space, and I had to find a way to figure it out. During my freshman year of college, I started going to counseling in response to childhood trauma that had begun to affect me (noticeably). I was in and out of counseling most of my undergraduate career up until finishing my Masters degree in Social Work. I told no one the full truth.

Honestly, I'm glad I took that route, because if I hadn't, there's a good chance I wouldn't be here today being able to share my story. It is a lonely feeling to go through life and face storms and battles that no one around you is able to see. It's not all their fault though. Many of us are masters at masking our true internal feelings and personal issues. As good as we are with it, it is not good for us at all; it just feels safe. As we see the increased rates of high blood pressure, mental health diagnoses, heart disease, and suicide, it's clear that the more we hold in the more we are hurting ourselves.

During my visit to Ghana, I learned that mental health problems and suicide are not a major issue in their country. I remember asking our tour guide why that was so, and the response was interesting but so simple; they talked to each other. The family unit is very strong in Ghana; family is the most important thing there. You'd be a fool to be a crook or do wrong by your family, because it is like a sin. With that, they have open communication. The families talk, have discussions together, and parents do not kick their children out when they turn *grown*. They live in more of a collectivist society; and neighbors are allowed to correct a child.

I didn't have that kind of open environment to share my thoughts and feelings. I don't think I really began to personally start living out loud until 2016. This was the year I decided to take myself back. This was the year I decided it was time to start living for me and only me. This was the year I promised myself to no longer suffer in silence when I really need a shoulder to cry on. This was the year I promised myself to be open and honest about my journey because that's honestly what I wish I had from other people. I went through most of my life thinking the people I looked up to were perfect; I thought they didn't have problems.

It's not that they didn't have problems, they just never talked about them. This is why I made the conscious decision to become more open about myself and my journey and talk about the things that aren't as pretty as my trips to the beach. As honest as it's told, I spent too much time thinking those trips were all forms of self-care, when in reality I was an empty vessel searching for something.

I was searching for myself.

I was searching for myself in the bottomless mimosas and all-inclusive resorts looking out over the ocean. I was searching for myself inside the self-help books I'd pick up in the store. I gazed through various forms of literature thinking to myself "Ooooooh this is EXACTLY what I need right now!" I know I'm not the only person who has gone through this or is currently going through it. This is the time for us to be honest with ourselves.

That's what it's going to take: Honesty.

Without first being honest about what the problem really is, we will find ourselves continuously searching for ourselves on an airplane, in a bottle, or in other people. I'm the last one to judge you if you can relate, because heck, that was me. So, let's be honest here. If you have ever felt like you weren't living out loud, what was holding you back?

We are all able to live a life out loud with confidence and humble conviction. It's not some secret club that is made for a select few people. Living Out Loud is available to us all, we just have to accept the challenge it takes to actually get there. Guess what? You're on no one's timeline but your own. So let the pressure take a back seat. We spend so much time looking at where we feel we "should be" or what we "should be doing" that we take away from our present moments and ability to see the power we have to create beautiful memories in our todays.

In my head, the more we each begin to live out loud in our truths, the closer we will come to a decreased amount of judgement and unhappiness in society. In this age of social media, we've gained more access to the world around us. We have developed a tighter relationship with virtual connections through the use of the worldwide web and platforms such as; Facebook, twitter, and Instagram. We honestly have access to EVERYTHING at the tips of our fingers. As good as this can be, it also comes with a lot of negative, unintended consequences. With the increased access to people and things comes increased insecurities and potential fear.

We sometimes succumb to the urge to compare ourselves to others whether consciously or unconsciously. Even the strongest person has fallen victim to this before; and it is ok. It doesn't mean that something is wrong with you; it just means that you are a human in your own right. It means that you have the ability to be reflective; we simply need to find a better way to channel the reflection.

That's all social comparison is.

We see where someone else is and may begin to question ourselves on where we are currently standing in life. We begin to reflect on things we may have done wrong or waited too late to pursue based on one post or picture. Or, we may even relish in the life we are living and find peace. Either way, another person's life story may arouse feelings inside of you. We may even doubt a person's happiness if we have seen them at one of their lowest or vulnerable points. We judge them based on our perceptions.

If we do not watch ourselves, we will be prone to fall victim to the alternative. You know what I'm talking about: The constant comparison and wishing that we were at a different place in life. The most successful people in the world may even find themselves wishing things were different. They may see a picture of a family sending their child off to school and wish they had spent more time with their own family. Or, they may wish they weren't always so busy. There is always someone wishing for something different.

I, personally, had to let it all go.

If we want to be ok, we have to LET IT GO! The way to do that is to become more comfortable about where you are and where you are on your journey. This is the time to be totally honest with ourselves, because if we don't, we will find ourselves continuously wishing for something different next week, next year, and ten years down the line. You want to know why? Because when we are unable to find the beauty in our journey, we are stealing away precious time that could be used toward fulfilling the dreams we have. The only reason I feel qualified to talk about these things is because I have lived through it, as well.

We all have a dream. We all have a purpose we hope to live out and fulfill. While some may believe that we are on an everlasting journey, there are also some people who have a bucket list; neither one is more important than the other. We have to identify our personal goals and visions for our life as we walk into our purpose; no one else can do that for us. While we are doing that, we must not forget the most important piece to the puzzle: Boundaries. Boundaries are key to us staying along the course. Boundaries are actually very tricky because they can be misunderstood. For example, I have been called selfish and rude for being assertive or maintaining a needed boundary.

Boundaries were necessary for me and my journey. They were instrumental in my development during the defining moments between life and death—literally. By creating boundaries, everything has become more doable and less overwhelming.

The goal is to allow us the chance to get real and go deep within ourselves and our current journey through anecdotes and learned wisdom. What are we doing that could be hindering us from walking in our purpose? Or, what are some of the powerful forces within us that are itching for a chance to come out and shine? By the time you finish reading this book, you will be forced to look at your life, purpose, and future differently. You will be able to look at others from a different viewpoint and identify when you are not living out loud as your best self. You will have a plan that is for you and only you. Well, if you approach it with an open mind, that is.

That is a topic I have experienced and had to learn and grow from. It always amazes me when people tell me they look up to me and how much they admire my work ethic. It's always crazy because I want to be excited by the statement, but my humility always brings me back to earth. I find myself talking to the inner me saying *they look up to me? Shoot!* If they only knew the hard work that has to go on behind the scenes. If only they knew the many failures I've had to endure in order to get to the place where I stand now. If only they knew the sacrifices that have been made with minimum external return. If only they knew the battles I fight daily.

If they only knew!

That is why I push transparency. I don't encourage people to believe that I am this high and mighty person who succeeds at everything she puts her mind to. I want you to see the real me. I want you to see those fears that have confronted me, those doubts that have made me anxious, those tears I have cried, and the work that is required 24/7! I'm not going to lie and say it is super easy, because it's not.

I want you to read this book with an open mind. As we journey, from page to page, I want you to remember that we are all human. Even wildly successful people have their bad times and have to work through them to get to purpose.

Chapter 2

When it's purpose-driven

Many of us may have read or heard of books that explore topics like finding and accepting your purpose. Most of those books approach purpose from a spiritual or religious standpoint, so it may alienate some from the journey. I personally feel they all have similarities. When it all comes down to it, it is dependent upon peace and understanding.

Before we get started in this chapter, I want you to think for a moment about your purpose. If you were to look at your life today, your goals, and future endeavors; what would you say is your purpose? Use the following lines to jot down what the word "purpose" means to you, and what you feel your personal purpose is in life, or purposeful moments you have experienced?

Now that we have that opening task out the way, I want you to try not to think about it again until asked. Trust me, there is a method to my madness with this exercise. Before we get deeper into your purpose, I want us to take a moment to dig into the word "purpose."

What does it really mean to live in your purpose? We hear so much about finding our purpose and following it, but there aren't many pieces that really talk about what a *purpose* is. If we were to take the Webster's dictionary definition of purpose; it is defined as an end to be attained or the act of being intentional. Simply put, it is something that can be considered destined to happen.

When we think of the term "purpose," we have been programmed to believe each person has one true purpose on this earth. That thought process alone has limited our ability to truly see all we are able to do and accomplish during our lifetimes. This isn't to say something is wrong with us, it's to show us that we are far more capable than we may initially imagine.

There are many books in the bookstore today that talk about purpose, finding your purpose, and living in it. One feeling you will most likely end up having is that you have to search for *that thing* that you are supposed to be doing. I honestly believe our purpose is not found in one thing, yet within a multitude of projects, relationships, and moments closest to you. What this means is that we are actually able to find purpose in all things when we control how we view it.

For example, I believe it was my purpose to be a social worker when I began my career, because it helped me learn more pieces to myself that I hadn't noticed before. It was also my purpose to travel to various destinations and meet the people I had the opportunity to meet because there was something gained from those experiences. Whether good or bad, I gained something that I hadn't had before; something that prepared me for the next step of my journey.

One of my all-time favorite books is The Alchemist. In "The Alchemist," Paulo Coelho, show through the main character the journey towards following your dreams. Along the journey, the main character, Santiago, encounters various people and things that force him to look within himself and various situations differently. This story is guaranteed to teach the reader the ability to find wisdom in all things and to see your journey and path as essentially one of a kind.

This is a book that I'd honestly suggest picking up to read once every other year. It helps keep things into perspective, especially when you have a bad day. Everything has a purpose. When I say everything, I mean EVERYTHING has a purpose. Even if we are just going off Webster's' definition, of reaching the end. When we do something with intention, it is considered purpose because we had a REASON why we did what we did.

I often suffer silently when someone tells me, "Oh my goodness you do so much! Why don't you sit down and choose one thing!" They do not all say it in those exact words; but the meaning is all the same. If you've never heard me say it before, you are hearing me say it today; I HATE THIS PASSIVE JUDGEMENT! Let's take a moment and break down what is really going on here.

They are first looking at the many roles I hold as being a burden and honestly doing too much. They are then basing what I do, against what they are currently doing as a way to make sense of my various roles. Lastly, they are applying the olden mindset of "you are supposed to find your one thing and do that perfectly." They may see me say here and there "I'm tired" or see I may not go to many social events or am in the house working on a Saturday night; so it may be assumed I'm not having fun. The reality is, I love all that I do. I love writing books, I love helping other people publish their books, I love learning, and I love making nail polish (it's like a self-care project). I honestly don't feel like I'm lacking.

But to people who are not on my journey, they see what they understand.

You will get some of the same reactions as you continue to go further in your journey as well. Do you want to know why? It's because many of us are conditioned to look at situations from our set of eyes. Not everyone is able to have an empathetic eye and can view a situation from another perspective of their own. It's a trait that is learned at a young age, and the older you get, the harder it becomes to grasp.

It's not impossible to learn, you just have to be open to being honest with yourself when you are wrong. Just like how many of us hadn't really started living until age 25, 30, 35, 50, and so on; it's a process to deprogram and then reprogram. The process is not always an easy one- but it is so worth it.

Now is the time to ask yourself, "Am I ready to live like this?" Living out Loud within your purpose is not an easy stance to take. On the days when you feel like your worst self, you have to show up the most. It's when we are able to embrace our bad days that we are allowed to fully appreciate the good days when they come.

So, what is really needed to live in our purpose?

Honestly, there is no long laundry list of items you must do before you are able to identify and live in your purpose. The only thing you really need to do is to alter the way you think. By realigning our mindset, we are able to change how we view various situations in our life. For example, say you are running late for work and you catch a flat tire. Naturally, our brains go to the fact that we are going to be late to work, which will then affect our payout/paycheck.

By changing how we view the situation, we are able to have greater control.

By looking at this situation as a purpose driven chance, a person may think to themselves, "I'm thankful this situation wasn't worse than this". The reality is, you could've been saved from a car crash or maybe you were purposed to have a conversation with the tow-truck operator. There could be various positives we can take from a negative situation in our life; but we just have to be open to see them.

Or, how about those bad relationships? I'll be the first to say, I have learned a lot from difficult relationships.

I dated a guy I just knew was going to be my husband. I was deeply infatuated with him because of how sophisticated he appeared. He had appeared in my life right at the time I admitted to myself that I was ready to begin a serious relationship. It all started off nice, like it always does in a relationship. We are always infatuated with the person in the beginning.

In the beginning, he would always call me queen and open doors for me. I later found myself opening my own doors again, and he began calling me Moe, no longer queen. Our disagreements began to turn into arguments, and eventually I began to feel silenced. I felt like he was my husband-to-be, so I went along with it. I'd be reflective, look at what I did wrong, much of which he voiced to me, and then I'd try to come back positively. But it seemed like nothing was good enough. Whenever I'd express that something was bothering me, he'd accuse me of messing up the vibe and being negative. It began to turn into a situation where it felt like I was pursuing his heart and he kept me by a string. Although he claimed he cared deeply for me, he never said he loved me.

It showed.

He swore up and down that he knew my love language; he didn't. It doesn't feel good when actions do not match words. Or better yet, when we ignore signs and write them off as being miniscule. It doesn't feel good to be pushed to believe that the things you have always felt made you beautiful weren't considered the same from the one you loved. It makes you feel like a caged butterfly, and it doesn't feel good.

One day it hit me.

I had been making excuses for our relationship. Every time I'd get flustered over something, I'd accept him telling me what I did and felt wrong; yet he never apologized for his wrongdoing. He'd ignore me for about a day, then come back around like nothing had ever happened. I was never okay with that and I had to accept that was him.

But it didn't work for me.

I had to change how I looked at everything. The old me would have viewed the situation as a failure on our pairing, but the reality is I learned something from it. I learned that I think deeper into situations than is needed. This doesn't work well with all people. To some, it can seem as if I'm too analytical and to others it looks like I'm *emotional*. Difficult relationships like this are a reminder of the importance of having a good friendship with your significant other. If you are not friends, then it will be hard for you to come together during the difficult times. Instead of coming together, you go apart.

That's honestly all that was needed: A change in perspective. The ultimate goal is to go to the affirmative meaning first, and not use it as an intervention to an initial negative thought. There will be times when you may go a long stretch with positive thoughts only; then something really bad happens. We fall down for a little bit, then get back up. Sometimes we get back up quite fast and other times it takes a little overtime. Whether a relationship or friendship, the process is still quite similar.

A couple years ago, I started incorporating something called Productive Affirmations into my daily routine. I would have an affirmation that I would commit to for that day, as a way to remain productive toward my work and interactions with others. I placed these affirmations in various places I frequented in my daily life, such as my bathroom mirror, bedroom, car, and office space. The ultimate purpose was to make sure I always had affirmative statements at the forefront of my mind at all times.

Positive and Productive Affirmations are all similar to the concept of conditioning the mind. They train the mind to view something from a particular point of view. I guess you could say they are a great way to reprogram your thinking processes. Examples of positive affirmations would be:
- Repeating bible verses for peace
- Talking to yourself; pep talks
- Vision Boards
- Daily inspirational memes

We see positive affirmations around us everywhere, honestly. They may be speaking to the tired mother, lonely single, grieving child, or even stressed out employees. You see them as you scroll through your social media and on billboards outside; they are everywhere when we are looking for them.

Did you catch that?

We see positive affirmations EVERYWHERE when our eyes are open to see them. Funny thing is, it doesn't matter where you are, they will be somewhere near. The only time we are not able to see these affirmations is when we are not looking for them or when we are operating with a negative spirit. When we are operating with a negative spirit, the glass will always be half-empty. To the positive spirit, the glass is always half-full.

Before we go further, I want to make sure we remain on the same page (pun intended). As stated, the goal is to allow our minds to see the affirmative sooner rather than later. We are all human, so of course we will not be happy all the time. I would be selling you a fantasy dream if I told you that you can reach the point of being happy 100% of the time. Honestly, there is no real fun and fulfillment in having the perfect life. The perfect life is without purpose. The goal is to find and see the purpose in each situation you encounter.

For example, my grandmother recently passed away- in February of 2019 to be more exact. That was the hardest time of my life growing through it. She was my best friend and the one person for whom I would do anything. We had spoken the night before she passed away and planned to continue our talk the next day. We really thought we would have the chance the next morning to talk; but life had other plans.

She was found unresponsive early the next morning.

I didn't realize that Saturday night would be our last time talking, which has left me replaying the conversation in my head. I was hurt. I was sad. I was angry. I was confused. It was hard for me to immediately see the purpose within what had happened.

Then one day it hit me.

I had been depending on my granny to be my emotional foundation and rock my entire life. She was like my best-friend and mother mixed together. Although we had such a close relationship, it honestly was crippling me because I had become dependent on her to be the hero in my autobiography. She was always my safe place. Whenever something bad happened, she was the first person I called. Whenever something good happened, she was the first person I called.

There was never a time when she was not available to talk. I'd call her house phone, cellphone, and repeat the sequence until she answered. That was our relationship and it was a comfortable one, because it is what made us the way we were. She is a major factor in my development as a person.

As much as I felt I still needed her, the universe had different plans: A new purpose.

In the midst of my anger, sadness, and hurt, I was able to see the sunlight within the dark clouds. It was my turn to finally step out and be those things for myself full-time. In the midst of this difficult time, I found purpose and beauty in what it could mean. So, what exactly did it mean for me? It meant that it was time for me to completely allow that little girl inside of me to get some rest. It was time for me to experience this sometimes harsh world without my comfortable safe space.

It was a reminder to me, that despite the different difficult situations we are forced to experience in life, there is always a purpose and rainbow at the end of the storm. I'd be lying if I said I don't still cry at her absence. I still allow myself to feel those moments of sadness, because it reminds me that I'm alive. The only difference now is that I am able to snap back into my present reality quicker than I was able to on February 24, 2019.

That's the real goal.

In order to fully see what purpose is, what it means, and how we are able to live within it; we must understand that it is not only found in the happy moments. Is that how you identified your purpose earlier in this chapter? I ask that because it's an important concept to explore. How we define and view life's moments have an effect on our life perspectives.

I want you to go back to the beginning of this chapter and re-read what you wrote about purpose. What did you write down? Did you look at the little moments or were they the big ones? Was it hard for you to find something to write? Has anything changed in how you look at it? Is there something else to your purpose that you may have not considered before? Now, I want you to take a moment and reflect on how you viewed your purpose and answer the following question:

In what ways have pain brought you joy and purpose?

_____

_____

_____

_____

_____

_____

_____

_____

_____

Chapter 3
When it's already yours

The good thing about all this, is that,
whatever is meant to be yours is already yours; you
just have to get it. That's the beauty of having the
option of *free choice* in the world. We are in charge
of what we allow ourselves to be and believe. Just
like one of my favorite poems, Invictus, states: I am
the master of my fate, I am the captain of my soul.

Life is not easy and it is not ever going to be
without problems. That is something we will
always know to be true. I mean, let's think about it;
what beauty is there in a life with no problems?
Without problems, what will we celebrate when we
overcome something? As good as it sounds, a life
with no pain or problems is hardly living at all.

It is lonely.

But that's not what Living out Loud is. To
live out loud is to live within your personal purpose
and journey despite what others may think or say.
It is to follow the pathway that your personal
journey has laid out for you with no regrets—even
though we make mistakes along the way. The
journey becomes more worthwhile when we accept

those mistakes and allow them to shape our future efforts.

This accounts for our dark times as well.

Going through a dark time doesn't always mean you have made a mistake or failed at something. Sometimes, you just find yourself going through a tough time that can't exactly be defined. We push through them by taking the needed steps and maintaining a transformative mindset. Although we may go through dark times here and there, it is our unwillingness to bow out that helps us win the longstanding war.

Many religions include the belief of a predestined life of prosperity. It's the belief that we already have a predetermined purpose in life; we just have to accept and follow it. This could make some believe that they do not have to do anything, to obtain that prosperity, which is simply not true. Whether you consider yourself religious or not, I do believe we can find something valuable from texts that speak of positive character. One of the most relevant is "faith without works is dead," a bible verse that is quoted often but rarely discussed in its entirety.

This verse is so strong when you look at what it is saying. We are often told that having faith that something is going to happen and keeping positive thoughts is the way to produce success. Unfortunately, that is not what is going to get us to where we are trying to go. We can want, think, and speak about everything we'd like to do and have; but if we aren't actively working towards it then we won't acquire it.

Everything takes work.

That doesn't mean we chase it prematurely or attempt to capture it, with no purpose. Just like the metaphor of the butterfly, it didn't land on me because I pursued it. I was pursuing it because I wanted to say I had a butterfly on my shoulder; there was no purpose in the reason. I can want the butterfly to land on me, but until I actually work on understanding *why* then the purpose is dead. All it is, is a want.

That is my take on life.

It is similar to the archetypes displayed in the movie, "The Princess and the Frog." Within its premise, it holds to the virtue that "all good things come to those whose heart is pure and stay true to their cause." Tiana watched her father talk about his dream of owning a restaurant her entire life, and she grew up wanting the same thing—to show off her cooking and keep the legacy of her father alive. She worked day and night, literally, in an effort to save up and buy the beloved sugar mill her father once fancied. She not only wished and prayed for the restaurant, she worked tirelessly towards it. Even when her mother tried to get her to slow down, she refused.

She was determined to reach what they both wanted most.

She grew up seeing her best friend, Lottie, have everything given to her that she desired while living in a very prominent side of town. She received all she wanted and all she dreamed of was marrying her prince charming. Despite the differences, she never complained, nor did it alter their relationship. She was focused on her personal situations and purpose.

Comparison is the thief of joy.

I want us to look at ways we can continue embracing our journey and allowing our purpose to live through us. I don't want us to look at someone else and look at ourselves from a place of deficit. I

want us to look in the mirror and approach our
growth with a strengths-based mindset.

I want us to see areas where we can let go of
control and allow life to take its course while we
continue working. Sometimes, we can have our
hands in so many pots that it becomes difficult to
devote 100% of yourself to either one. We must be
able to delegate and trust others to work within their
best selves and take some pressure off of ourselves;
it's imperative. That's what letting go of control is.
When we let go of control, we are creating
expectations, boundaries, and aiding in someone
else's experience and development.

Throughout this book, we've had the
opportunity to reflect on certain pieces of our
personal selves and have been allowed to dig a little
deeper than the surface. We've basically gone
through the process of learning how to accept life
and things around us. I don't need to know what
you wrote, neither does the world. The only thing
that matters is that you have accepted it for what it
is and have allowed yourself to find power in the
moment.

Acceptance is the major piece to the puzzle.

As we are constructing the picture of our feelings, goals, and purpose we must always remember to L.I.V.E. It's a process that we get better at, the more we do it. To L.I.V.E. is to live, identify, validate, and erase. Here is a quick break down of each:

1. LIVE in your personal truth
2. IDENTIFY and reflect on past failures
3. VALIDATE and find balance within your life
4. ERASE fear

As you can see, they all relate to what we've discussed throughout the book. They are all an important piece of the process and journey. Each of our stories are different, so how you go through your individual process is going to be relative to you and only you. We all start at a different line and that is just the way life is.

Live in your personal truth

If you don't take away anything else in this book, my greatest hope is that you take away the importance of reflecting on your personal truths. We can't live out loud if we are unwilling to accept our personal reality. What this looks like is starting the process of analyzing those controversial parts of your story. Are their pieces of yourself that you have kept buried because of how it looks to others? Are there things that you have refused to acknowledge within yourself?

Some of us are carrying secrets inside that we have attempted to hide from ourselves. Even though we feel it is the best way to let it go, it is important to acknowledge them as being a part of you and your journey. Your truth is your truth. No one else has the same life print you have and that is what makes it all worthwhile. Each one of us have the right to feel special because of biology alone. There is no one else like you, and there will never be.

Living in our personal truths also means tackling the toxic habits we may have developed. It is imperative for each of us to look within and find what toxic behaviors may display in situations. The tricky thing about toxicity within behavior is that it is subjective. What is considered toxic in one personal relationship can be received as healthy in another. For example, some people may like direct communication from someone; but others won't. Sometimes, our behavior can cause unwelcomed feelings to arise in another person, which can negatively affect the relationship.
That's why I said it is tricky.

To be honest, most times, it is a mixture of both people not understanding each other or how to approach the situation. But, when both of them are living out loud within their personal truths and are in-tune with each other, they are able to communicate their needs. When we are able to communicate our needs then we can have healthy interpersonal relationships. That's why it's imperative that we live out loud. The more we accept ourselves for who we are, the more we can experience in life.

Identify and reflect on past failures

This is a major one! I know many of us were raised to look at the present and ignore the past, but I believe that can do us some disservice sometimes as well. Many researchers and sociologists believe that the past is the window into our future, and it depends on whether we leave that window open or closed.

I truly believe when we leave the windows of our past open, we open ourselves up to learn and grasp our present reality. By closing out and choosing to not acknowledge those past failures, we place ourselves at risk for repeating those same mistakes that can be bypassed the next time around.

I can speak forever on this topic, because I have been somewhat hard-headed in my past and even sometimes now. At the end of the day, shutting out our past failures is ok for short term coping, but it harms us in the long-term.

A great way to reflect can be the use of a journal or blog. Some people are ok with having their personal feelings displayed for others to see; others or not. Personally, my deeper feelings have been written in my journal and reflections are posted on my online blog. When we are reflecting on something, it is important that we ask ourselves the following questions:
- What happened?
- How did I react? What was the consequence of my reaction? What did I change?
- How did I feel?
- What did I learn?

By organizing our thoughts and feelings, we are able to make the most value of our personal experiences.

All in all, be willing to forgive yourself and move forward. We are primarily haunted by the consequences of our past actions because we hold onto them through unforgiveness. We are always taught to forgive others when they do things that hurt or we don't agree with, but we never hear people talk about the importance of forgiving ourselves. So many of us are walking around with unforgiveness in our hearts because of something we did in the past.

We hold ourselves to such a high standard, which isn't a bad thing; it's actually a pretty good practice. We should want to always be our best. Unfortunately, this can also become bad when we hold ourselves to such a high standard that we don't allow ourselves to be human. We blame ourselves for getting something wrong, for failing at a project, for choosing the wrong intimate partner, etc. We become so upset with ourselves that we continuously hold it over our own heads. We are our own worst critics when it comes to making a mistake.

My plea to you is that you stop being so hard on yourself. Allow yourself to be human, make mistakes, and learn from them.

Everything has a purpose in our life—even our failures.

Validate purpose and find balance in your life.

After we have given ourselves the opportunity to forgive ourselves for those past mistakes and reflect on them, it is time to push into that purpose. This comes after our reflection because if we are walking around with unforgiveness in our heart, we will be unable to see past it. Everything we think about and do will be a reflection of our internal unconscious perceptions of reality.

When it comes to validating our purpose and finding balance, we are basically identifying where our passion lies. This is the time for us to think about when we have felt the most purposed. Where have you found your heart strings pulling you the most? What feeds your soul? What type of work and projects drain you and which ones energize you? These are questions that help us get to the answers we seek.

Unfortunately, finding our purpose is the easy part. The hard part is finding balance in our lives as we juggle all the responsibilities we have on the day to day. The majority of us reading right now have multiple roles we play. We are a parent, spouse, student, co-worker, owner, daughter, son, and siblings; we are someone to so many different people. On top of that, each one of those roles have responsibilities that come with them, such as doctor's appointments, parent/teacher conferences, birthday parties, work schedules, meetings, homework, and exams.

Most of us who are reading this right now are plain ole tired, and I don't blame you.

That tiredness comes from a compiled list of work and unwelcomed energy. The only way we can really battle tiredness is by finding balance. It is important that we find balance for our peace of mind and pursuing our goals. We find balance by identifying areas where we are wasting time. Finding balance in our life is similar to balancing a budget. We decide we want to start saving for a family vacation, which means the money has to come from somewhere. With these new goals, we begin to move around our budget and savings goals in order to develop the perfect plan.

The same thing goes for your passion and purpose.

The most important tool for keeping balance in your life is the use of boundaries. Boundaries are extremely important, especially for those of us who interact with many people or have demanding occupations. It becomes so easy to lose ourselves in the never ending list of what needs to be done; while attempting to show up for everyone else. Sometimes, we can't do it. Sometimes, we're going to have to be unavailable. Its ok to cut that phone call short if needed. Its ok to tell someone you can't make an engagement.

It's ok to say no.

Erase Fear

This is the final and secret key to living out loud in our purpose; despite other people and obstacles. Fear is a dangerous thing that we can carry around inside us. It's silent, yet it affects our decisions, our actions and inaction, and it dictates our actions without announcing itself. Fear is embedded in us. We often shut ourselves down before we even take a step forward. We begin to question how it will be received by others, and if it will be successful.

Where fear resides, hope is unwelcomed.

Before writing this book, I was in the same boat. I had begun writing it around the time I started writing "They Never Told" but I had always been hesitant on finishing and releasing it. Although I loved the topic and felt it was helpful for others, I asked myself if other people cared. In reality, I was afraid. The fear of it not being well-received, like my most popular book was, loomed over me. This is honestly something that many authors go through; we hope to be as successful as our first book. The same thing hit me. It was through different conversations with my friends that I realized this was a book that people wanted to talk about, and I needed to check myself back into reality.

So many of us have allowed the fear of repeating past mistakes to push us to uncertainty in everything we want to do. We begin to doubt ourselves because the fear of failure haunts.

So many of us have developed these fears from past failures and hurts. But, when we address them and welcome them for growth it becomes easier to push through them. It's time to let them go. I know many people feel as if they are motivated by their fears, but external motivations can affect you both consciously or unconsciously.

Erase your fear of time. Yes, that is correct, the fear of time. This is something that most of us have dealt with at some point in our lives. Heck, some of us are still dealing with it unknowingly. This fear of time and visions of an imaginary race against time pushes us to believe we are not where we 'should' be. It tells us that we don't have enough time to do that thing. It tells us that we are not ready because it hasn't been enough time. Time literally dictates most of our movements.

It's time to say goodbye to fear and the only time we need to focus on is now- right now.

It's not only time to say goodbye to fear, it's time to LIVE! It's time to start working towards those goals you have inside of you. It's time to start working on that business plan. It's time to start living for you.

Chapter 4
When you're finding your purpose

Many of us have lived lives that have been confusing for others to comprehend or understand. We have all made decisions that made people look at us weird or accuse us of making a bad decision. I, for sure, am no stranger to this plague as well. I honestly can't blame them, because if I didn't know myself, I'd confuse my identity along with everyone else's.

I have tried and accomplished so many things. Some things I have done would be considered inter-related and others weren't. If you were to look at my resume, you'd honestly ask yourself how it all ties in together- because, to the closed-eye, nothing looks like it fits together. My entire life's journey may look disconnected to one who is not open to see the connection. Still, it made sense.

It made sense to me to quit my job and go back to school for my Masters of Social Work.

It made sense to quit my job in the mental health and substance abuse field and go into teaching.

It made sense to get my Masters of Education.

It made sense to quit my job in teaching and pursue my Doctorate in Education.

It made sense to write my books.

It made sense to create a nail polish line I believed in.

It made sense to braid hair when I wanted to.

It made sense to work at a factory before heading to Michigan State.

Heck, it made sense to donate plasma when my cash was low.

It all made sense to me even when it didn't make sense to anyone else. Honestly, if I didn't have faith in myself, I wouldn't have been able to jump off the cliff into the unknown so many times.

I'm glad I did though! If it wasn't for the supportive and loving faces around me who never allowed me to beat myself up, I wouldn't have built that confidence. The fact of the matter is, despite how small or how big some of my roles appeared to others; they each held an important purpose in my life until expiration.

Just like your first job. You always hope to move up, but you also know the relationships you build are worth it. During my time working at McDonalds, while in high school, I was able to make money to support my activities in school, to manage having a car, and I met some of my closest friends who started off as just co-workers. Those friendships have been fruitful during the years. One of which, was instrumental in my success at Michigan State; she was like a big sister and good friend to me.

Even though my purpose now is to hold McDonald's accountable for their food practices, treatment of workers, and wages, I also appreciate the time I spent there because of the social capital. That's what I value most; the relationships that are built in different settings and situations. It's hard to operate in a toxic environment with people you can't trust.

I've had those situations before. Those situations where you have found your co-worker in the middle of a lie far too many times, yet you have to continue working with them. It becomes difficult to maintain peace within the environment. My grandmother used to always say that life is 10% what happens to you and 90% how you react to it. That factor never really made sense to me until I got older. NOW, it makes perfect sense. There were plenty of situations I found myself in where I wanted to curse someone out and pop them upside the head. I'd be lying if I told you that I didn't!

But, I can't.

Now, don't get me wrong… I could easily reach over and pull a wig or two off; but it's the consequences that I do not want to endure. When you know your purpose, it makes you double back when you want to do something that may not be the best option. I have spoken my mind before, and they knew how I felt; but just know my venom could've been more deadly.

But it's not always worth it.

That's why I want us all to be able to see, identify, and work within our individual purpose. Sometimes, we find ourselves in situations that contradict what we are supposed to do because we operate outside of what we should do. I've fallen victim to this, and it's my goal to keep more of us from continuing to make this mistake. No matter how hardcore some people are, when something bad is done, I do not think their purpose or intention is to end up in jail even though there is a good chance of it happening. I know that is a little extreme, but I want to convey that our purpose is defined by the potential consequences.

This is a concept I work to teach my students every day. I see them behaving erratically, and I don't judge them; I was once them to the extreme. Thank goodness Facebook wasn't around until my freshman year of college. My Facebook memories would be popping up with some inappropriate posts by me. I know this, because I know I was a handful. Although I was on the honor roll, received many scholarships, and experienced life, I was a total mess and many didn't know. As I look back, I know most of those behaviors were attempts at getting attention and the result of lack of emotional intimacy from my upbringing. As a counselor, I get that now. I was seriously messed up in the head.

That's what I want the youth to get as well: The sooner we learn it, the better.

I truly believe we find purpose in the middle of difficult situations more than anywhere else. Difficult situations harbor difficult decisions, and difficult decisions require intense thought. When you are deep in thought, the purpose is to see all perspectives of the situation. Our purpose is not something we simply find, it is something we experience. The problem with the premise of having to search for your purpose is the belief that it is not already within you; that it may be alluding you. When you find something, it is assumed that you were either seeking it or you found it by accident. I don't think this is a good way to look at identifying our purpose.

Our purpose can be compared to chasing butterflies. We see the butterfly floating around and we want it to land on our hand or shoulder, so we begin to chase it. We don't realize that the more we chase it, the more it eludes us. No matter how hard you try, the butterfly will most likely refuse to land on you. It's their way of telling you "you're doing too much and you're not ready!"

That is what I feel like the butterflies at the Niagara Falls conservatory told me! I remember walking through the enchanted butterfly garden, in awe, as I watched the birds and butterflies fly and flutter by. As I walked around, I'd see butterflies landing on some of the kids' shoulders and all I could think about was one landing on me. I have always been in love with butterflies. Their life process tells a story and is representative of how we should view life.

The more I found myself trying to get the butterflies' attention, the less I noticed them flying near me. So, instead of continuing my persistent pursuit, I decided to just walk through and enjoy the views. As I walked, I found myself viewing the scenery and becoming present with just being in such a serene place. I wish I could end this story with a happy ever after, as I explain the feeling it was to finally have a butterfly land on me; but I can't. A butterfly never landed on me and I didn't get a chance to experience the magical feeling that is supposed to follow.

At least not at that time.

You see, it was my trip to the gift shop after, that gave me my epiphany. There was a wall plaque I noticed as I was exiting the shop. There was a quote from Henry David Thoreau etched in it:

Happiness is like a butterfly, the more you chase it, the more it will evade you, but if you notice the other things around you, it will gently come and sit on your shoulder.

This quote is very powerful because it ties into identifying, finding, and obtaining your purpose. You see, we can focus all our time on the end goal that we miss out on the work that has to be done prior to. It's when you pay attention to the work you must do towards obtaining your purpose that it comes to you.

It was this quote that helped put everything into perspective. I was preparing to leave my first salaried position, after almost three years, to pursue my Masters of Social Work. In the midst of the transition I had so many other things going on at the same time. I wanted to do it all and I wanted to reach the end goal. This quote reminded me about the patience that's needed when we are following our purpose.

Contrary to popular belief, I'm actually an introvert. I have to hide away, alone, to gather myself when I feel overwhelmed. It takes a lot of energy out of me to be around a lot of people for long periods of time. When this happens, I usually take a trip away somewhere—preferably someplace near water.

My trip to Niagara Falls was all about self-care and finding balance between my passions before starting school. I made the decision to quit my job and go back to school, so I decided on a mini trip in preparation to get mentally and emotionally prepared. Niagara Falls was only a 3 ½ hour drive from Detroit, so I bought a hotel on Priceline and made the drive across the border. The trip felt destined, when my "name your price hotel" turned out to be the Tower Hotel, and my room had the best views of the falls. I literally slept with the blinds open as I scanned the glass windows that stretched from one end of the room to the other. When I travel, I typically request a room on a high floor so I can sleep with the blinds open. I love watching sunsets and sunrises; they provide the most peace.

Purpose found me, when I stopped looking for it; just like butterflies. I found peace in my decision to leave a full-time job and step into the unknown. Although I knew it was something I needed to do; I was still slightly uneasy. The butterfly didn't land on me at the conservatory, but the revelation and peace in the unknown let me know that it's only a part of the process and journey.

After this trip, those things that stressed me out as I was preparing to transition I didn't worry about by the time I made it back home. I didn't begin every project that I wanted to do at that time. I found peace and reminded myself to not stress over what had yet to come. The strength of the falls, as our boat rode across their horizon, reminded me that I could face any challenge that came my way as long as I remained true to my path.

Over the course of my life, I have overcome many things. If we were looking at my past statistics, you'd never think to see me where I am now. I guess you could say I beat the odds.

All in all, the reality is, we will never be perfect at living out loud without tests and trials. There is no person who is always happy. Happiness is a homemade emotion; it is created. Through that creation, right there at the heart of it all, is our purpose which is fed by our passion.

One day, I was having a disagreement with someone and they blurted out, "You don't even live like you post!" and it honestly left me slightly confused. Those who know me know I share both good and bad moments that happen in my life. So, I was baffled by the comment. But then it hit me. I believe the human mind has become trained to see the good things first and sometimes ignore the "not so pretty" things that others share. Because of this selected view of reality, it is easy to see a person for how you choose and not the reality. Interestingly, this is not the same thing when we look at ourselves. We tend to look at the negative aspects first.

Earlier in the book, I stated that one of the goals is to have our minds assume the affirmative/positive aspect sooner than later. That doesn't mean we become insensitive to things that are negative or unhappy. Unfortunately, that's what most of us do. So many of us spend so much time scrolling the internet and wishing certain areas of our lives were different. So, what do we do in response? We block out those things we do not want to see or those things we don't understand. By doing this, we begin to create this false understanding of people and miss out on learning about all of them.

I have not always felt full of purpose. A lot of my life was spent wishing I had different circumstances. As an outcast, it was hard to feel included in various circles and my confidence was often shot down. I have gone through my MESS years. I have also not always been considered innocent. The reality is, I know I have probably been the topic of a few people's therapy session (and not in a good way).

So, what's the real news?

I have made many mistakes, and I'm a mess just like everyone else. We have to get the vision of this perfect person out of our heads. By us having this vision, we begin to have this false sense of self and projection of the potential future. It's simply not realistic. When we do this, we are keeping ourselves from enjoying the true beauty of our individual journeys.

As I look back, I think my personal truths are what helped me become so open-minded. I'm less likely to judge someone else. Rather, I try to learn WHY. Even if it pisses me off, initially, I eventually reflect on the moment. Don't get me wrong, just because I'm open-minded, doesn't mean I accept things that are toxic to my growth. Empathy is not allowing someone's brokenness break you; it is understanding the *why* and creating healthy boundaries. The reality is, we all have a village that is built for us. It may not be a family member or best friend from kindergarten. On the other hand, it just may be; it just depends on your personal tribal needs.

Some of you may be wondering what exactly I mean when I say your village. Don't worry, I won't leave you hanging, we are going to get into that in the next chapter. I don't know where I would be without my village, so that totally deserves a chapter in itself.

You see, there are so many pieces that go into the puzzle of identifying and living in your purpose. Some parts of the path may be easier to identify than others and that doesn't make it any better. Just like my lesson with the butterflies; don't spend all your time chasing them. Allow your truth and energy to attract them.

Chapter 5
When you find your village

I think we are at the part of the book where many are excited to know what is coming next. You want to know how I know that? Well, research says the human attention span is quite low—eight seconds to be exact. What this means, is that if something is not showing me a different image every eight seconds, I begin to lose interest. I stand by this statistic, just based on my personal experience. My attention span to something is sometimes very low if I'm not introduced to something different.

Before I get to the next part, I will say, this problem with our attention span and patience is also something that gets in the way of us being able to see our purpose.

I won't go too deep into that yet, since it could be a whole book in itself.

I want to change the pace a little bit. We've gone over a lot of concepts in the last three chapters, and I want us to stop and do some reflecting. Honestly, there is no true change or understanding without reflection. As an educator, we are trained to do something called "checks for understanding." These checks for understanding can come in the way of a quick question or even an assignment as review. Either way, it is important for us to make sure that what we are saying is getting through and making sense.

I've learned so much over the course of my life, both professionally and personally, that has made me look at many things differently when it comes to walking in my purpose. I guess you can say they are life lessons and skills that make living much easier.

These life lessons are all reflective of lessons I have had to learn through interpersonal interactions, personal reflections, and professional endurance. The reality is, it is not easy to play multiple roles and carry so much weight to make sure each role is carried out with accuracy and efficiency. I have always had a strong appreciation for parents, specifically mothers who carry multiple roles.

It's not easy.

Let's take a moment and think about all the roles you currently play. How do you know when you're almost overwhelmed? What do you do when you are tired? Who do you talk to when you are having a bad day?

_____

_____

_____

_____

_____

_____
_____
_____
_____
_____
_____
_____
_____
_____
_____

I'm pretty sure most of us have seen those memes and articles floating around with the title of "check on your strong friend." The concept was pretty revolutionary, if you ask me; but it had a negative consequence as well. I don't think we really thought about the probability of everyone feeling like they are the strong friend. So, instead of reaching out, they expect someone else to reach out to them. Because the reality is, in a good friendship, no one should be wearing the other person down.

The truth is, we ALL get tired.

We all get tired sometimes, it just shows in different ways. In our friendships, we should be present for each other when one is down and the other is up. If we don't have that, it's imperative that we find it somewhere.

I was scrolling Facebook, one day, and I came across a shared post that showed a man applauding his wife for her multiple roles. She was a full-time student, full-time employee, full-time mom, full-time wife, and she had a baby on the way. I don't think her husband meant any harm when he posted the picture applauding his wife, but the Facebook world found concern with the entire scenario. There were people who were upset at him for not noticing that his wife may be severely fatigued. There were also people who were making comments, such as "what does she need you for?"

The interesting thing was that I found myself understanding all of the arguments being made. Often, we applaud someone for persevering through difficult situations. Or, said another way, we applaud people, most often, when they overcome a difficult situation. We like to applaud the outcome or should I say the picture of achievement: the end goal. What about during the process? In this scenario, we don't know what type of relationship that woman has with her husband, and it's not our business to know. But, what we can get from the situation is that we need to make sure we pay attention to each other when we are going through our difficult times and storms.

Our minds are trained to reward the finish line, so it can become difficult to pay attention to the journeys of those around us. We know that we are going through trials and experiences, but we may not always give that same thought to someone else. It is not that we think we are the only one who goes through difficulties. It's just that we don't always reach out to someone to check on them. Or, we continuously expect someone else to make the first move to reach out not realizing they may be struggling as well.

It's so easy for us to internalize our personal problems and isolate from others when we are feeling overwhelmed. It has become easy to do this in our society, due to how busy we have all become. It has become easy to allow a couple months to pass before speaking with a close friend. It has become convenient to write in our journals instead of returning text messages. It has become normal to cut off people.

But the rate of anxiety and depression is increasing.

I found myself asking the question of "why?" more often than not when it came to anxiety and depression. Not because I didn't understand it, but because I wondered why we are getting away from each other the way that we are. Those who have read my blogs know that I have lived with anxiety and depression in my lifetime and was even suicidal in my teenage years. There's something about a firsthand experience that can alter your perception of something. I realize that when I am going through anxiety, I begin to worry. When I begin to worry, I try to isolate. I say try because that was a characteristic I chose to overcome. I no longer isolate when I am going through my moments; I reach out to my village.

That's why it saddens me when I look at how far we are getting away from human communication. Most of our communication is had through a phone or computer. Don't get me wrong, when you are long distance from people you love, having a phone or computer available is beyond helpful. But, it may not be a good idea for us to use that as our primary form of communication; especially when we live in the same city. There's something about human interaction that can be therapeutic when we are around the right energies.

Yes, the right energies.

I truly believe that we become what we surround ourselves with. If you surround yourself with negative people, you will eventually find yourself becoming more negative. If you surround yourself with criminals, you find yourself guilty as an accomplice at trial. The same thing goes for the opposite side. When you surround yourself with people who see the glass as half-full, it can help you keep a positive perspective. This isn't true always, but in most cases it is. Sometimes, a person can be so toxic, that it is hard to rub off on them; they actually begin to influence everyone else.

In those cases, RUN!

We need those positive energies of human communication. I took a psychology class during my senior year of high school, at the local community college. This psychology class was an introductory level course that looked at social interactions and the foundations of human psychology. The instructor shared, one day, that human energy can be transferred through different pressure points of the body. This transference of energy was said to even be able to aid common problems, such as headaches and strained muscles.

This concept was so cool to me.

Having someone with the intuition of healing hold their hands near your pressure points can be all someone needed. It was that class that deepened my appreciation for naturalistic healing and made me want to learn more about natural healing through interactions. I constantly found myself performing what I learned on people who'd complain of headaches.

This just goes to show the importance of human interaction and communication.

That's what a village is. By definition, a village is considered a community with shared beliefs and values. We may see villages in different African Countries or within indigenous groups when we are reading a book or article. It is basically a close, organized group of people. Your village can be made up of family members, friends, colleagues from work, or even classmates. There is no required timeline for someone to join your village. For some, your village may consist of a best friend.

Let's take a look at my primary village. My village is quite diverse when looking at the various personalities and energies it provides. My village is a group of people I feel I can come to in my most vulnerable state and they not only hear me—they see me. I can talk to them about my fears, my goals, and my accomplishments- and neither feels more important than the other. Opposite of popular belief, your village doesn't have to be only your best friends. Some may link them in this same category, but I personally don't.

Truth is, I don't share the same beliefs as my best friends, so there are some topics that I stay away from depending on what the intentions are. For example, we do not share the same religious beliefs, so I most likely won't call them for advice on spiritual matters. Instead, I talk to someone in my village who I feel can connect better on that topic.

It's like my village provides a sense of peace when I feel misunderstood. I have my village for school, my village for career, and my village for life in general. Each village member is more than an associate, they are essential to shared mutual support and advocacy for development for one another.

This is why I strongly suggest we all have a village.

When we are being faced with difficult situations or group dynamics, it's beyond helpful to have your village near to keep balance. For example, I have had a village for every school program I have completed. We shared the same stresses and responsibilities of being in school. We were able to relate on many things because we were living through similar situations. These were the people I contacted when classes were feeling too hard, the people I study late with, or who I have girl's night out with. My village and I have an understanding: I am there for them and they are there for me.

I guess we could put it this way, your village is made up of representatives from different sectors of your life. You find your village in different ways.

My villages helped me get through difficult break-ups, drunken college nights, deaths of loved ones, celebratory moments, and disappointments. My village have been motivating, encouraging, honest, and accountable. I can think of a thousand times when people have come through for me in various ways. I'd be a fool to think I've gotten where I am on my merit alone. A great lesson I had to learn was that there are more people willing to help you than people who aren't. Far too often, I have grown victim to thinking about the people who hurt me or didn't support me.

By giving them my energy, I was taking available energy away from somewhere else that deserved it.

It's not fair to our better selves to feed the negative more than the positive. It hurts when it feels like people aren't rooting for us or supporting our causes. It's ok to feel the feelings that come with it, but it's not ok to dwell on it. When we dwell on it, we are putting our available energy into something that is not fruitful.

Let's look at this scenario:

When I released my book, They Never Told, there were quite a few people who hadn't supported as I expected them to. I'm talking about people who were in my circle who I supported and expected to support. I call them the people *I rode hard for*. It wasn't even about people who hadn't bought a copy; some of them didn't even come to one of my book signings. There were some who claimed they had no idea I had a book- even when I know I told them personally. It all really hurt. I found myself thinking about it after each signing. I'd go through the whole process of asking why they hadn't supported me and carefully analyzed each situation.

And guess what? It was DRAINING!

One day, I was talking to my granny about my feelings and being upset. Her response to me was a major key. She shared a very important lesson that I needed to be reminded of. I needed to stop focusing on who didn't show up and appreciate the ones who did. That made so much sense. I had become so critical of myself and others because they hadn't showed up that I hadn't put sufficient time into the people who were present. It's like another form of customer service, honestly. That day was the last day I allowed my focus to be given to someone who doesn't *see me*. When I say *see me*, I mean, they are able to see and appreciate me for who I am and not who they want me to be.

I came to learn that by focusing on the people who were present, it also helped my anxiety. The reality is, as a child I grew up very insecure, and I had an attachment problem. Seriously! I used to follow behind my cousins, because I didn't have a lot of friends and people I felt comfortable around. Up until around the age of 11, I used to follow behind my older cousin. Part of it was because I always wanted an older sister and the other part was because I thought she was cool. I wasn't a cool kid in school, in fact my siblings and I used to get teased a lot.

The school my siblings and I attended in Monroe, MI was a diverse school. Although it was majority white, there were kids of other races present as well. We weren't one of the more privileged families at the school, and it often showed in our clothes and the activities we participated in. I can still remember the first time we were called the "stankin besters" and I went home and washed our clothes in the bathtub by hand; I made sure to spend extra time on them that day.

The basement of our one-bedroom home had flooded and our clothes and belongings were primarily kept there. We didn't have a washer and dryer and our water was sometimes cut off, which usually meant my brother and I had to get water from the side of a neighbor's house. As the oldest child, there were a lot of responsibilities that were placed on me with regard to my three younger siblings.

I always felt responsible for them and was not allowed to have a normal childhood. If something happened while my mom was gone, I got in trouble. When we didn't have food, I found a soup kitchen for us. When I wanted to play with kids outside, my siblings had to accompany me. This is honestly a scenario that many kids have to live through today, and it's not fair. It's not fair for parents to place such a responsibility on their children because it's convenient. There were so many things I had to deal with in silence, because I felt like no one cared to listen to me.

So reading was my getaway.

And visiting my cousin… even if it meant riding with her pedophile father to get there.

My cousin and I had a love for the boy band, Immature. Both of us just knew that Romeo was her man and Batman was mine. We'd collect word-up magazines and sing our hearts out to them. I remember she had this 8-ball that I would always play with. Besides the many hopes of one day being rich, I wished for love and friendship.

That's why I always followed behind her. I didn't see her current struggles. Nor, did I see my mom's. I was just a pawn in the unknown realities.

After I moved with my father at the age of 10, I started following behind my other cousin more. Before moving to Muskegon full-time, I visited during the summertime; during which I'd be following behind her and vice versa with my other cousin when I moved with my dad. They were like the big sisters I never had—even if it meant suffering a little in the process. Sometimes, I would wonder if they liked having me around as much as I liked being around them. I focused on the negative and the feelings of rejection. These attachment problems I later found were related to different life experiences.

I was insecure.

And anxious.

I still sometimes have anxiety, but it is manageable because I am able to notice and prevent it from spiraling out of control. That anxiety is not the same around people anymore. I realize when I begin to tense up, it is because something is off about the interaction. It checks me to make sure I am being my best self and to make sure I am paying attention to the energies around me.

To those who may feel there is no one out there who gets you or who will understand you. I'm here to tell you that there is, but we just have to feel and understand the interactions ourselves. Although, I had heard the lesson of paying attention to those who are present before, I needed my grandmother to remind me of the importance in that moment.

It may have been because of the depth of They Never Told that made me emotionally connected to it. The topic was a sensitive one, so it was expected to be important to everyone else as well. It's hard to talk about sexual assault, let alone share a part of your own story while writing others' as well. It can be expected that people around you are supportive of the endeavor; but that is not always the case, and it is unhealthy to assume it to be. I can go back and forth thinking about all the time I have lost from focusing on the wrong things, but that won't do me any good either. It's best to just reflect on it and let it go.

What honestly got me through the process was my loved ones who stood there with me during the entire process. It was my grandmother's nightly prayers and random messages of love and encouragement. It was my mom keeping my dog for me when I needed to transition. It was my dad sharing his wisdom. It was my friends encouraging my endeavors. It was my will to keep going.

That's why I had us do our reflection earlier. When we are thinking about our village, we have to think about the people we trust most with some of the most vulnerable pieces of our hearts. Whether it is our village at our job or the people we talk to for advice, it's important we don't try to go it alone. It's critical for us to notice when we are on the verge of being overwhelmed because it is easier to be preventative than reactive.

Just like the metaphor of broken glass. It can be put back together, but it will never be seen without its cracks again.

So, how can we stop the glass from being broken? We have to first make sure it is protected from the potential of falling and have a safe landing available in case it does fall. Because guess what? Falling is oftentimes inevitable.

Chapter 6

When it is hard

One day, one of my Facebook friends posted "I'm just playing, I don't want to be a grown up anymore!" I felt exactly where she was coming from! Though it was a joke, it had so much real-life context within. As kids, we go through so many disagreements with our parents and the structure of education that we find ourselves wishing we were grown up, to only wish we no longer had the responsibilities we are now accountable for.

Life can be so hard at times. No one is exempt from facing the random occurrences and experiences of life; no matter how pure your heart is. Even when it gets hard we have to keep going. It's so easy to stop when we are faced with opposition and you seem to be the only one rooting in your corner. It feels easy to give up. I want to share a little about my history of writing and a time I stopped.

I remember one day I had gotten so upset with my dad. When I was about 14 years old, I was big into writing in my journals still. Not only did I like to write song lyrics and poetry, I would write about my inner thoughts and feelings. Everything that kept me going and stable was written down because that's how I found my solace. Well, one day, my dad found out I had a diary that was gifted to me from his ex-girlfriend, Tina. It was a new password journal and he overheard me talking about my password.

He started going into this spiel of how he had the right to read and see anything in his house as long as he paid the bills. I tried to reason with him and told him that it was my inner thoughts and feelings, but he disregarded them all. When the conversation was over, I told myself I would just keep the diary at my granny's or my best friend Monica's house instead. The reality is, I stopped writing my personal thoughts as much. I was afraid that my inner thoughts and feelings would be revealed to someone else.

I couldn't wait to be grown.

Lo and behold, I started back writing my freshman year of college when I was on my own. Even though this was the beginning of my complete independence, I wish I was more prepared for dealing with hard times. Even though it was hard, I still had to learn it. Life was not going to stop for me to figure it out. I had to take what I had been given and grow from it the best I could.

Being an adult is difficult, especially when you have the responsibility of being a parent and/or spouse and our actions affect other people. Because of this truth, we are destined to have difficult times.

The important piece is how we get through the difficult times when they happen. How do we still make the best decisions even when we are faced under pressure? Just like I discussed in an earlier chapter, happiness and purpose is found in overcoming difficult times. Just as much as you, I hate the difficult times and wish they were no more; but that's just not the case.

But, what if I told you that isn't entirely true?

Honestly, a lot of what we go through can be avoided by making better decisions. I know this one firsthand. Just think about the different red flags you have gotten in situations that you chose to ignore, to only later wish you had paid attention to it. I know I have done this in relationships and ex-friendships more than once. Instead of listening to my intuition, I usually allowed reasoning to take over to later regret it.

I could have easily saved myself from the hurt that later followed.

One of the main problems I've come to see in our way of thinking as a society is that we have the mindset that we are supposed to continuously go through tough things in order to get to our happily ever after. Seriously?! How many times have you seen relationship quotes online that talk about going through storms, not giving up on your partner, and loving someone through their toxic behaviors? We have begun to normalize the struggle, which makes us numb to it in such a way that we sort of seek it out, rather than grow through it. The struggle mindset keeps us in deeper struggles.

It would be wrong of me to criticize only our society; we have each accepted this concept— well at least those who refuse to see it. I have stayed in some relationships that should have ended long before they really did. I know I'm not the only one. I just want you to think about the moments in the beginning that may have warned you of behaviors that led to why you ended. It's not about dwelling on what went wrong; it's about learning from them to do better next time.

Reflection Time: Think about a time when you were your worst enemy in a situation. What did you do? What didn't you do that you should have done? What would you do differently?

_____

_____

_____

_____

_____

_____

_____

_____

_____

_____

_____

So, why is it really so hard to walk in our purpose, as adults?

It's like the older we get, the harder it becomes to step off the ledge and take the leap of faith needed. We find ourselves making some of the same mistakes for years straight and continuously telling ourselves we will "start tomorrow." We say things like:

Tomorrow, I'm going to start working out.
Tomorrow, I'm going to give my grandmother a call.
Tomorrow, I'm going to stop and get gas before work.
Tomorrow, I'm going to wake up early and do it.
Tomorrow, I'm going to start that paper.

Putting things off to tomorrow is our enemy. We put so much weight on tomorrow that we become disconnected from today. We make it harder on ourselves by putting the expectation of tomorrow on us, before it is even here.

So, let's get to the root of why it's so hard. Why is it so hard for us to take the few extra moments and do those things today? I think fear is one of the major culprits.

One of my favorite poems, is by Marianne Williamson. In this piece, she talks about what keeps us from becoming our best selves: She simply shares that our deepest fears are not that we are not good enough. Our deepest fear is that we are even greater than we expect ourselves to be.

Who are we to continue procrastinating on what can better us? We know what we should be doing, because our heart string pulls us, but we find a way to reason with those feelings. For lack of better words, we make excuses. The reality is, by taking a few minutes to get your gas after work, instead of before work tomorrow, you're able to have time to read a chapter in your book in the morning, or you may be avoiding the potential of waking up late and unexpected traffic. By starting your paper tonight, you're making room in case something happens to your computer or you get sick around the time of the due date. By calling that person tonight, you remove the guilt of potentially no longer being able to talk to them again the next day.

I wouldn't be telling you this, if I hadn't learned from each of those lessons before. I have lived and experienced them all and there is no reason to beat myself up about it. Especially, since I listened to the lessons instead of ignoring them.

Why wait for tomorrow to do what you can do today?

This message came to me in a dream one day from my Granny. After my granny's passing, I was going through intense grief, and I had been praying that she would appear in my dreams. I have vivid dreams a few times a week, so I found myself praying that she would show up in my dream each night. Frustrated, I realized those prayers weren't working.

It seems like she waited until the night I didn't cry myself to sleep to appear to her baby girl (me).

In the dream, someone and I (I don't remember who) was at her house in her back room hiding. As a way to hide, I was laying on the floor along the bed. My granny kept coming into the back room trying to talk to me, and I kept telling her to wait until the people were done searching houses.

She didn't care.

When we got word that they were no longer searching the neighborhood, I came out to talk with her. As soon as we went outside to talk, I dropped my phone and it broke. My grandmother told me in that moment, "Why wait for tomorrow to do what you can do today?" This is the message she left for me.

You see, I was the last person to speak to her. The last person to hear her voice.

I called her the night before she was found unresponsive. Unfortunately, she was really tired and said her throat was hurting, so we weren't able to talk long. We made a promise to talk the next day since she planned to stay home from church. 41 seconds is what I have left of her. 41 seconds to soak up her voice. 41 seconds to share our love.

I could have easily said, "I'll call her tomorrow" after I got home late from campus. But I didn't because I wanted to hear her voice. I'm glad I listened to that inner spirit.

But, that's not my truth in all areas. Although, I'm not as bad as I was before, I still have some growing to do. I still allow my tiredness to interfere, at times. I still allow procrastination to rear its head here and there. I still allow myself to fear what may happen in the unknown. But, there are people who still believe in me and I still believe in myself, so I keep catching myself when I fall into the trap.

This takes us back to the poem by Marianne Williamson. Our greatest fears are not that we can't do something, it's actually the opposite. Our fear of making the right choice includes the expectation of greatness and that is what scares us. But, why should we be scared if it's the journey that matters anyway?

We shouldn't fear developing ourselves. We shouldn't fear the potential of a friend holding us accountable. We shouldn't fear the mistakes we have yet to make. We shouldn't fear failure.

We should welcome the potential it all brings for growth. We will make mistakes along the way; it's inevitable. But, it's never ok to make the mistake of not trying. There is no foolishness found in trying.

You know, getting to a place of contentment hasn't been easy—for me at least. To be content and find peace in your truth, you must first accept that which is your truth. In one of my favorite movies, The Titanic, Rose stated "A woman's heart is a deep ocean of secrets." That statement has always stayed with me because there is no lie found in it. We each walk around with so many secrets buried inside us that no one knows about, except us and our higher power. Even though we may have a best friend whom we share a lot with, there are still things we keep to ourselves.

We carry around deeply rooted fears, insecurities, behaviors we aren't proud of, regrets, and wishes we hold close to our heart—in silence. Well, at least it is silent in the auditory context, but they are still affecting us internally. The more we ignore it and bury it down low, the more we are robbing ourselves of personal freedom. Instead of admitting to ourselves those feelings, we deny them or make excuses for them in order to have them make sense.

I'm here to tell you: you can't truly live out loud without facing those difficult thoughts. I want us to take a moment and do a personal survey. Before we move on, we are going to reflect on our internal truths and secrets.

Reflection: What pieces of your life puzzle have you chosen to keep to yourself? Is it a relationship with someone close to you? Is it something you have done or the fear of what might happen?

_____

_____

_____

_____

_____

_____

_____

_____

_____

_____

_____

_____

I want you to really think about what you wrote in your reflection. It's going to be instrumental in your process of living out loud—trust me.

Ok, are you ready for my vulnerable moment? Before I go into it, if you're not ready to read one of my hard truths, I suggest you skip the next few paragraphs. It may make you look at me differently. Not that I care, I just know that everyone reading this book is not ready for the true concept of living out loud, and that is ok with me. What is not ok with me is allowing yourself to endure something you don't feel you're ready for.

Ok, so now that the disclaimer is out.

One of the deepest secrets I carried around with me was my love for sex. This may seem somewhat disconnected, but bear with me; the story has a purpose.

It took a long time in my life for me to accept the fact that I loved sex. I'd be intimate with my partners and feel guilty about my wants; so I became very insecure. Oddly, the more insecure I became, the more I wanted it; it was quite weird. It wasn't until the day I finally admitted to myself that I loved sex and I loved the feeling it brought, that I was able to fully enjoy the experience. Since admitting that truth to myself, I was honestly liberated. I became connected to my femininity and I began to become one with myself. You see, it wasn't the partners or actually the act of sex that pushed me; it was my connection to the true feminine inside.

I grew up in a strict Christian household, so things like sex weren't discussed. I was always told to not have it because it was a sin to do it before marriage. After being violated so much before the age of 10, sex didn't have a particular meaning to me. I just knew I started early, and I did it: A lot. The only person who ever talked to me about it, died when I was 14 years old, so after that, I was on my own and what I learned from my social circles and HBO after midnight (with my TV on mute).

By freeing myself from the miseducation and internal confusions, I was able to take back my power. I became more secure in myself, which showed outwardly, and I was in-tune with my better self. This truth not only set me free, it allowed me to gain access to the next level of self-actualization. I no longer cared about being judged, I was free. I knew what I liked, what I didn't, and I had no problem letting you know. I was living in that truth and it was no longer hard to face.

Although, I am celibate now, I am still powered through my femininity and confidence that was gained from accepting my sexuality. I tell myself now, if I am blessed to one day have a daughter, I will teach her to accept and embrace the beauty of herself. Not only from a sexual perspective, she will learn that she has a voice and her feelings matter in all areas of her life.

We often fail to teach young girls that their thoughts and feelings matter. They are not always being taught that they have a voice and that it matters. It's deeper than sex. It's society not sexualizing us for what we are able to do and to appreciate us for what we have done.

By teaching our young girls how to love themselves properly, have confidence in their individuality, and how to live in their worth, we are telling them that they matter and that their truth is a safe space. They don't have to struggle to get to that point. Let's keep it real. The main reason why so many of us ladies have carried on this secret competition with one-another or internal doubts is because we weren't given the freedom to grow through the journey as little girls. So then, we find ourselves in our 20's, 30's, and 40's trying to heal the little girl inside of us.

Finding and following our purpose doesn't have to be hard, but for many of us it is, especially, when you aren't given the tools needed. The good thing is that it's never too late. We just have to be willing to put in the hard work that is required of us. We must be willing to ask ourselves those difficult questions and get to the heart of our soul's deepest secrets. It's time for us to face our personal fears that have been keeping us from taking the leap of faith. It's time for us to see the beauty in being grown and utilize those perks and opportunities for our good.

It's not an easy task to change everything you have been taught or learned mindsets. You literally have to create a new meaning for everything around you. It will be slightly difficult, but it will be worth it. The joy we get from following our purpose supersedes any difficult moments because we are connected and aligned through our truths.

Chapter 7

When it's meant for your harm

We each have a testimony!

I mean that so much, that I have to say it twice; WE EACH HAVE A TESTIMONY!

We all have something to be happy and excited for, because we know what the alternative outcome could have been in each situation and experience. We know what bullets we have dodged and how many acts of mercy we have been granted. I know I for sure have been the recipient of some major grace, favor, and mercy. I know I have also been the recipient of interacting with some just plain ole mean people.

You see, every good thing is not good for you.

I was having a talk with my co-worker one day about being positive in situations. I shared with her that I would like to have a fairly positive experience with everyone I encounter, but there are times when my intuition and/or energy isn't at ease with them. It's so hard for me to give the benefit of the doubt to something or a situation that gives me the wrong feeling.

Don't get me wrong, the situation may be perfect for her. But, if my alarm goes off, I investigate the feeling. I want to know when the feeling arose, what happened to cause it, what the feeling is, and what it is saying. I want to know it all so I can make an informed decision. More often than not, my intuition turns out to be on point.

It's the times when I didn't listen to it that left me wishing I had.

One of the greatest mistakes we can make is expecting other people to think and act like we do. That is a set-up ready to let you down. Everyone we encounter do not have our best interests at heart, nor do they all want to see you win. I'm sorry to be the bearer of bad news but, there are some bad people in the world. There are some people who are so damaged that their purpose has become ruining others along their path. One of the realest things someone could have ever told me was, "They are not all happy for your sis!"

The reality is, they aren't.

What's even crazier, is that "they" are most likely not a stranger. "They" are usually people who know you and have most likely known you for a while. "They" can be your family, friends, associates, and sometimes strangers. Honestly, I don't think most of them know what they are doing when they do it. Remember what I said earlier in the book. So many people look at others through the lens of social media and other accomplishments and begin to compare. Sometimes the comparison can be good, but most times it is not.

The same way that person has never clicked "like" on your picture is the same way a person can snub you from a promotion you deserve or that "best friend" can gossip about you to someone else. We are a threat to their current existence. It is hard for an unhappy person to be genuinely happy for someone else; it takes a pure soul that everyone does not possess.

Sadly.

What makes matters even worse, are the times when someone tries to sabotage your purpose. People like this find everything they can to steal your joy. I don't think they all do it on purpose. But, I do believe it is inherently embedded in their hearts. Some people have love in their hearts, and some people have hate. That's just the way the world turns, unfortunately. They aren't always trying to snub you; some just don't know how to operate through love.

What helped me start looking at these situations differently was changing my perception of their "why." By changing how I viewed them, it helped me gain a better perception of what was really happening. It doesn't change how I feel about them, but it keeps me from wanting to curse them out.

Here's one of my testimonies. One year prior to me deciding to actually submit applications for Masters of Social Work programs, I was planning on applying to Eastern Michigan University (EMU) for their program. They had a two-year, part-time program that would allow me to commute between Lansing and Ypsilanti for class. So, in preparation for submitting my application, I reached out to my potential recommenders in advance.

Now, EMU required that you send all the components of your application together—including your references. After notifying my references of my intention and asking if they would be willing to provide a letter of recommendation, I sent out the requirements along with an envelope for them to enclose and sign over the flap. Somewhere between the time of sending out my references and receiving them back, I decided I no longer wanted to apply to EMU. They didn't have the full macro concentration in policy that I was hoping to get experience with, so I decided to wait and find a different school.

Instead of throwing out my materials, I sat them to the side and didn't think about them.

The next application cycle, I decided to apply to Wayne State University in January 2014. They had a greater macro policy focus that I was seeking and was more aligned with my goals. In preparation for this application, I asked different people for letters of recommendation. Not only did I get into the program, the Dean of the College agreed to be my faculty advisor!

Alright, so let's back it up a little bit to the heart of the story. While I was in the process of packing my apartment to relocate to Detroit, I came across my application packet to EMU. After reading through my personal statement, I came across one of my recommendation letters. This letter was provided by my supervisor from my internship with Big Brothers Big Sisters. I had no intention of opening the letter up previously, and EMU didn't require you to waive your rights of anonymity, so I was greatly intrigued.

So, I opened it.

I couldn't believe my eyes as I read the scores given to me on the Likert scaled questions, then down to the qualitative assessment. I was learning how she really assessed me. Later, at the end of the recommendation, she checked that she didn't recommend that I be admitted into the accelerated program. My jaw instantly dropped!

This is a woman whom I had daily work consultations with and who provided updates and grades to my internship liaison at Michigan State. Not once did any of her concerns come up during our time together. If she had a concern that big, she could've easily used those moments to teach me; but she didn't. I was honestly hurt as I read her comments about my lack of passion and inability to succeed in a program; she actually had no faith in me. It was this day, in 2014, that I realized that everyone who smiles in your face is not really in your corner.

Not only did I go on to be a Masters Level Social Worker, I graduated with an 'A' cumulative average, helped start and run two social work-student campus organizations, and was selected to be The MSW Student of the Year with the National Association of Social Workers- Michigan Chapter. What she meant for my harm still turned out for my good as I realigned with purpose. I was never meant to attend EMU, and I was meant to read those comments. I was meant to see exactly how some people saw me.

What is meant for you and your purpose will always be there for you no matter who tries to get in the way. This isn't the first time I encountered this type of behavior and it won't be the last, sadly.

That goes for you too. There are going to be things that happen in your life that aim to throw you off balance. There are going to be people who get in your way and do not have your best interest at heart. There are going to be plans that don't go as scheduled. Let them all happen.

Because, what is for you, will be for you!

As I think over my life story, if you were reading a book of statistics, it would tell you that I shouldn't be here. It would tell you that I am supposed to be somewhere barely living. It would say I am not worth the risk. It would suggest that I am just another statistic. But that's not the case.

You see, you and I have both gone through copious amounts of hurt and bad times. Times that some people are unable to get back up from; but we did. Not only did we do it in the past, we continue to do it on a daily basis. You may have survived growing up with an addicted parent, abuse, sexual assault, poverty, severe mental health, backstabbing, debt, and emotionally unavailable adults. You may have survived being in the wrong place at the wrong time, being somewhere you shouldn't be, and being there for people who aren't there for you. You may have survived absent parents, neglectful partners, inconsiderate jobs, and skyrocketing costs of living. I've lived through it all, plus some.

Guess what? We are still surviving.

That's what following our purpose is about. It's about allowing those moments that are meant to harm us the opportunity to teach us valuable lessons. The hard part is accepting what that lesson may be. My grandmother used to always say that sometimes God puts you through the same trials until you finally learn the lesson you're supposed to find in it before you are given more. This makes so much sense when we think about the popular saying…

To whom much is given, much is required.

If we can't prove ourselves worthy with the amount we have been given now, how can we expect to sustain more?

It's time we stop feeling so defeated all the time. We are stronger than that. Ok, you didn't complete that goal when you wanted to. Or, you didn't get that job you interviewed for. So what, SO what, and SO WHAT!? People go through trials every day. What sets those who walk in their purpose apart is that we see it as a stepping stone toward something better.

I'm not saying become a robot. We are allowed to feel sadness in the moment as well. There is this meme going around social media about Beyoncé. The meme says that she allows herself to feel deep sadness for 24 hours after something happens. After that, she gets back to work and leaves it behind her. I'm even happier that this is in reference to Beyoncé, because I often find myself asking WWBD?! Of course that means, What would Beyoncé do?!

I respect Beyoncé's work ethic to the max!

What we can learn from this, whether she said it or not, is that it is ok to feel the feelings; but don't stay there. After a while, if you aren't careful, that sadness turns into pity.

Just think about what it's like being a black person in America. We know the various struggles and hardships our ancestors have had to endure. The forty acres and a mule that was promised us has yet to arrive at our doorstep and it seems like more and more of our youth are being criminalized before they even learn how to walk. Despite how many may feel about the black plight, it is very hard.

But guess what??

There are too many of us weighing on that and allowing it to be a crutch as to why we aren't following our passions, purpose, and goals. I know I may be ostracized by a few for saying this, but I have thought carefully and intensely about the topic. My visit to Ghana solidified what I had been feeling for quite some time. Many of the things that have been created around us are the same things that are aiding the crippling mindsets we find within urban communities.

Slavery is one of the worst acts one can do to mankind, next to murder and rape. We have gone through all three of these as a people; around the world. But, for some reason, some of us utilize the opportunities given to us more than the others. Although Africans from different regions, were taken to the Caribbean, South America, and North

America; none of them work and hustle the same way.

It's amazing to see the work ethic of black people across the diaspora. We have it here in the USA too, but it is not as common. We have higher rates of drug addiction, mental illnesses, and homelessness found within our communities than other areas of the diaspora. We are also more individualistic as a people compared to others who have more of a collectivist approach. We have helped build a capitalistic society that is breaking us down at the same time. We see each other as competition vs. a friend with whom to climb the ladder. As much as I want to accept the crabs in a barrel explanation or house slave mentality, this is not common across the entire Trans-Atlantic slave trade diaspora.

Maybe, it's because our oppressors stayed in the same country as us. Or, maybe it's because we have become more like them. Either way it goes, we need to do better.

We need to love each other more.
We need to correct each other more.
We need to support each other more.
We need to work with each other more.

These have been my observations after traveling to many countries across the world. It baffles me how young adults can scroll through their phones all day, complain of being bored, but wishing for thousands of dollars. Do you not realize you have all you need in front of you to begin? We should never be bored when we are working towards something greater. Everything we do should be with intention, reason, and purpose.

It's time for us to get up and use the lemons we have received to make fresh lemonade that your haters will one day pay you to drink.

Chapter 8

When boundaries are needed

This is probably my favorite chapter thus far, because it allows me to get to the heart of things. I have faced much opposition from people across my life; my family, friends, sorority sisters, classmates, and romantic partners to be exact. I have heard my fair share of comments about how I am too loud, I'm too ghetto, I'm uneducated, I'm too black, I'm too emotional, I'm not the right fit, and so on and so forth.

If I calculated the ratio of positive interactions and negative, I truly believe I have been told more about my negative attributes than my positive ones. When you are different, you become an instant target to neutralize. What is even worse is when their complaints relate to something you love about yourself. How do you really combat that? Many of us shrink ourselves to be smaller and unnoticeable. Others reflect and make meaning out of the complaint and begin changing things about themselves. Then you have the few who decide to fight back. Finally, you have the group who carefully considers other people's intentions and understanding.

I have played each one of those leading roles before and none of them felt quite as good as the one I'm living now; living with personal boundaries became an absolute must.

I found my family and romantic partners to be the hardest to fathom my evident difference and unclear goals. It's like I never made sense. My butterfly spirit was like a threat to their security and my entrepreneurial spirit made others reevaluate their lives. I didn't ask to have this impact on them; my mere presence did it for me. These clear indifferences and misunderstanding poured into various relationships.

One of my ex-boyfriends had a problem with my lifestyle. He never said it directly, he would always make little comments about me being famous and like a butterfly. He'd make comments about the clothes I chose to wear and my public personality. It was hard for him to understand that what I chose was always for me and not for others. Just because I post a picture on my Instagram and it may attract random guys to comment, I am never swayed by that and I felt he shouldn't be either.

We just didn't mesh and I realized we both had things we were working on. The problem with it was that our areas of healing clashed. When you clash, it will be hard to hear and understand someone. As bad as it may feel, it's all ok, not everyone is meant to be in your village.

It wasn't my purpose to heal him. It wasn't my purpose to be his therapist in the moment. It wasn't my purpose to stay around while negativity flew throughout the relationship. It wasn't my purpose to appease his insecurities that would sometimes turn into emotional abuse. It wasn't his purpose to understand or attempt to heal me. It was my purpose to have healthy boundaries and do what was best for me and my physical and mental health. At the end of the day, we just weren't on the same page. Our journey's and purposes were different, and I wish him well as he continues along the trek to figuring it out.

It is so easy for us to get caught up into this picture of what we are supposed to be doing, what it is supposed to look like and how it should be done. Unfortunately, that's not exactly how life works. I mean, it can work that way if you choose to allow it; but I can tell you now that you won't be fulfilled. There were times that I went along with things to keep a person from walking out of my life or criticizing me for my choices.

But then I became secure and unafraid. I became my biggest fan.

I became so aligned with my purpose and secure in my abilities that I could no longer accept less than what was due me.

It was during my super insecure phase where I dealt with cheating boyfriends, parents censoring me, jobs micro-aggressing me, and disloyal friends—in silence. I was remaining silent and losing myself in order to stay in line with their narratives.

I was suffering the most.

And it wasn't fair to me or them because there was no accountability.

Boundaries are so important when we are talking about interacting with other people. They sound like they are easy to create, but believe it or not, a lot of us have a problem with creating and maintaining them. I mean, even the word "boundary" sounds complex. We see boundaries every day in life, we just may not notice them all. Boundaries can be defined as a limit or lines used to divide or block off. So, for example, the lines dividing each driving lane is considered a boundary. It tells the driver, "This is your area and the other side of the line is someone else's." Other examples of boundaries are stop lights, state lines, fences around homes, etc. There are a lot of boundaries in our lives that help keep structure and order.

The easy part is setting the boundaries; the difficulty comes in enforcing them when they aren't respected.

We can easily say, I'm turning my phone off every day at 8pm to read a chapter of a good book before bed. The difficulty comes when we are scrolling our phone at 7:58 and come across a really interesting article that we want to read. So here you are, now, at 8:05 reading the comment section. Just that quickly, your set boundary becomes lost and you put it off until "tomorrow." We can say we will break-up with someone if they are ever found cheating but find ourselves in a five-year relationship with a cheater and manipulator. What happened?

I think fear is the first culprit in this situation—the fear of making the wrong decision, the fear of not being understanding, the fear of not having the life you imagined. Fear is the killer of many dreams. We find ourselves straying further and further from our true selves in an attempt to mold into what is needed, wanted, or expected of us. It's not always on purpose and that is how we break out of it.

We have to become aware of our triggers, our boundaries, and our fears.

If we are not aware of our personal fears and triggers, we will continue to be a slave to them. As a slave, we will be unconsciously controlled by them without knowing. Fear is a dangerous feeling even in its simplest form. Our fear stops us from seizing the opportunities we have yet to encounter. Fear of trying and not succeeding, fear of trying and succeeding, and fear of trying and losing interest controls the daydreamer's mind. The way out of it is truly learning and developing yourself—what triggers certain reactions in you and what boundaries you should strengthen.

Once we become aware of our deepest fears, which include triggers, we will then be able to set boundaries that work for us. Before then, we will find ourselves continuously going back on a boundary we set. When we become aware and learn to see certain traits it becomes easier to maintain healthy standards and boundaries with people we interact with. For most of us, that may mean going to therapy to get a better grasp of things.

That's absolutely fine.

I am a strong advocate for therapy. The saying, "Life is 10% what happens to you and 90% how you respond," is totally true. When it comes to setting healthy boundaries, we can't expect to change others. We have to become our best selves and teach others how to function in our lives. We basically have to teach people how to love us. The difference is knowing what role they should have in our life and what boundaries are best. The boundaries you set for one person may be different than the ones you set for someone else.

For example, there are some people who have a severely negative spirit.

Every time I talk to them, they are always focusing on what is wrong in their lives and the lives of others. Now, I understand that there are going to be hard times in our lives, and we won't always be happy. But, I also understand that I am sometimes like a sponge; I soak up energies around me. When there are people like that in my life, I have to scale out how often we have conversations and when is a good time to end the conversation.

The same thing goes for us. We have to be aware of how much we are putting onto other people. It is okay to vent to our village, but when we begin to notice it is all the time, we have to seek professional support. It is not fair to put this all onto our village who have their own problems. We oftentimes give advice based off our personal situations and perceptions. In the case of therapy, they are trained to teach us how to solve our own problems, without them just giving us advice.

It's an internal process.

Boundaries are the bridge between you and peace. Sometimes, a boundary doesn't look so pleasing. For example, sometimes, I have to pass up on hair appointments because the potential client's available time doesn't work for my schedule. In the past, I would sacrifice some rest in order to accommodate. I can't do that anymore. I know the difference of my energy at 12noon vs. 5pm and that awareness holds me accountable to everything that is on my plate. If I miss out on rest today, that will affect my full schedule for tomorrow. As my schedule is affected, the feelings of fatigue can negatively affect my mental health and ability to solve complex programs.

Sacrificing our boundaries can be like a house made of dominoes.

The shift of enforcing boundaries is very similar to the mindset shifts that occur with going on a diet. It is difficult in the beginning, because we are seeking the same tastes we received with the foods we no longer eat. The only things that can help with following the new habit is time and continued determination. I grew up hearing the phrase, "it takes 21 days to form a new habit, and one day to break it." The good thing with enforcing boundaries is that when you mess up, it's ok to forgive yourself and try again next time.

So, you're probably reading this chapter trying to reevaluate your current boundaries and assessing if they are still working for you or not. These areas can range from romantic relationships, friendships, habits, professional endeavors, educational needs, and mental health. Are you aware of what you need in order to be your best self? Are you familiar with areas you should have boundaries? If not, that is going to be the first step to identifying and growing with healthy boundaries. How well do you know yourself? Let's take a moment and check it out.

- *What are the signs that you getting tired? How do you look? How do you feel? How do you act?*

_____

_____
_____
_____
_____
_____
_____
_____
_____

- *How much sleep do you need to get in order to wake up feeling refreshed?*

_____
_____
_____
_____
_____
_____

- *Explain when you feel least motivated and/or productive?*

_____
_____
_____
_____
_____
_____
_____

- *When are you most productive?*

_____

_____

_____

_____

_____

_____

_____

- *In what areas do you feel you should focus on building boundaries? What is taking the most from you without significant return?*

_____

_____

_____

_____

_____

_____

How did it feel to write those out? Were you honest with yourself? That can be hard sometimes, especially if we are made to feel guilty because of different roles we hold. One of the largest marginalized groups are parents. Although I am not a parent, I have studied hundreds of parents and their behaviors. I have watched parents who are entrepreneurs, parents who are college students, and parents who are in the working class. One of the common things I noticed is their love for their children and their development. Even when it comes to sacrificing their personal goals in order to do so. I'm not saying this is the wrong to do, but what I am saying is that if you want to do more, then you have to work harder to do what you want while still showing up for your child.

Society has made it hard for parents to feel comfortable about following their goals and dreams while raising a child. They tell you this is your time to do x, y, and z, and forget that you are still a real person. You still have real feelings, goals, and visions. Who said you can't do it all? We see it all the time with proper supports.

One thing I have learned from watching goal chasing parents is that they are fiercely disciplined with their boundaries. They have a color-coded calendar and schedule that is planned out in advance. They have a village whom they are able to lean on when needed; and they accept the challenge of following their goals and purpose. I'm almost sure none of them would tell us that it is easy, I'm also sure we won't hear them say that it isn't possible either.

The truth is, no matter what roles we are currently holding, we can be working toward our purpose and goals at the same time. Let's move away from just looking at the big picture and where we want to be. As long as we are moving forward, we are moving in the right direction. That's the beauty of following our purpose and goals; there is no rule book on how we should do it.

We just do it and continue to learn, organize, strategize, and grow along the way.

As you reflect on your responses to the questions earlier in this chapter, I want you to make sure you are being honest with yourself. The answers to those questions are starting keys to making sure you are developing and maintaining healthy boundaries. By knowing your triggers and best working conditions, you are able to properly plan. Although bad things can and will happen, the more prepared and flexible you are, the easier it is to get through.

Chapter 9
When you find peace in failure

I don't care what anyone says, there is no ultimate rule book on the pathway to success. Each of our pathways are personal to us and cannot be duplicated no matter how many blog posts or books we read. There are some people who can step out into their personal journeys or purpose within business endeavors and find success within six months. Meanwhile, for others, it may take upwards of a couple of years to see the fruits of their labor. Although we could be working on similar projects our pathway is different and will always be different. We each have different connections, skills, and references that may place us in different places with different opportunities.

This is why marketing and reading blogs on successfully building a platform can be a little disheartening at times. You may find yourself following all the tips to identifying an online presence for your business through social media and other prospective ways. A couple months down the line, though, you find yourself getting upset and wondering why your online engagement is not picking up. You think about the different pieces of marketing advice that was shared online and begin wondering what you may be doing wrong; you just can't seem to figure it out. You start to compare yourself to the author of the blog you're referencing or you scroll your timeline and see someone else in your field flourishing.

This is an area where I can speak from experience. I have gone through the process of building a non-profit organization and for-profit businesses. I know how it feels, to feel like you have failed. Heck, when I first entered business, I quit a couple times because it was becoming too much for me. It wasn't that they weren't a passion of mine, it was just super hard, and I couldn't get a grasp on marketing and the making money part of it. The truth is that you can have all the passion in the world, but it still can't be used as payment on your electric bill. Anyone who owns a business wants to make money, and you can only make money with good marketing, contacts, and customer base.

Period.

This same thing applies to other passion and purpose projects. There is not a one-size fits all method to success. Success looks differently for different people.

This is why it is important for us to have our own identity for ourselves and our business. I had to learn this. It is ok to marginalize a few in order to target your preferred group. Its ok for you to say that your products are for women of color or women with blonde hair. If that is your audience, then that is your audience. Even when you are working with your audience, you are still going to have some failures. I have so many stories of failure that I can now look back on and laugh about.

For example, if it wasn't for mercy, I probably wouldn't be here in this moment right now. My freshman year of college could easily have been my last year of college. The transition to a new life was far from easy for me. I thought I knew what to expect when I left to go off to school, to later find that I was a stranger in a new environment that I knew nothing about. I didn't have parents who understood going off to college or completing FAFSAs, so how could they really help me transition into an environment they themselves weren't familiar with?

They couldn't.

Unfortunately, my high school didn't do a good job of preparing me either. Even though, I was the girl who graduated sixth in her class and accumulated the most in scholarship money amongst my classmates, I almost didn't make it out of freshman year. My first semester of college, I earned a 1.4 cumulative GPA (grade point average) for the semester. Anything below a 2.0 GPA at Michigan State places you on academic probation. So, putting two and two together...yes, I was on probation. It didn't stop there though; the next semester, I managed to pull off a whopping 1.1! At this time, I was required to have an academic counseling session to see what was best for me at the university.

I met with my academic advisor and we talked about my options. Typically, you are allowed to remain on academic probation for two semesters, and then you are dismissed after the third semester. During one of our meetings, we discussed career options. At this time, I was a pre-nursing student so I had science and math courses on my schedule primarily. He had me take a career assessment and it recommended I look into social sciences. This is when I was introduced to the field of social work.

I was intrigued.

So, we came up with a plan. I'd take summer classes to get above the 2.0 and register for social science introduction courses; such as psychology, sociology, and social work. This was my final chance to reach a 2.0 GPA. I worked diligently that semester to do better and I did. But, better was not enough to get me to the 2.0. My summer GPA was a 2.75 which brought me up to a 1.6. I did better, but not good enough.

As I started walking towards my advisor's office door, I was anxiously awaiting him to tell me it was time to pack my bags and go back home. We looked over my transcripts, the classes I had taken over the summer, and classes I was planning to take in the fall. After looking over my documents for what felt like ten minutes, in silence, he returned to the conversation and said "I'm proud of you."

I was shocked.

That was the last thing I expected him to say at that time, heck I was expecting to be kicked out. He continued to note after retaking my algebra course, I increased my grade and showed that I am able to do the work. He stated although I didn't make the required shift, he noted great progress and had faith I could pull it off with one final mercy semester. That is exactly what I called it, because it was the extra semester I wasn't supposed to get. I am aware of some of my peers being kicked out of the university for the same thing I was going through; but they weren't awarded the same mercy.

It hurts to see how unfair some things in life can be, but this also pushed me to get my head back into school and see it for what it should be. This failure turned around to be my motivation. I never got back on academic probation, graduated with a 3.5 GPA in my major classes and a 2.8 overall. I was proud of that because I know where I came from. I went on to graduate school where I earned a 3.9 in my Masters of Social Work program and a 4.0 in my Masters of Education program. I promised myself I would continue to push myself to learn and excel in what I do. I am not ok with just doing enough to pass; I want to exceed the basic requirements because I know I am not a basic person.

That's the role our failures should play in our lives.

Our failures should be seen as a stepping stool to get us to something different and/or better. We take what we learn from the experience and apply it to something different. My failing forced me to learn new ways to study, plan out my schedule, and push for more. It goes back to earlier in the book when we talked about finding beauty in the pain. Our passion and purpose can only be fulfilled outside of our comfort zones.

Period.

We can only achieve greatness by stepping out of our comfort zone—similar to the journey of the caterpillar and butterfly. The caterpillar has to step outside of its comfort zone and turn into a cocoon. The interesting thing about the cocoon, is that while living inside there is limited mobility available. Whenever it rains, snows, or is ruffled by strong winds, there is nothing it can do to protect itself. It withstands it all. As it withstands the harsh realities of nature and life it is rewarded with transitioning into a beautiful butterfly.

It's imperative that we do not praise the butterfly and ignore the caterpillar; they are both important to the journey.

I want you to take a moment and think about your personal journey. Share your experience with a moment when you felt like you failed. Consider these questions: What was the failure? What happened after the failure? What did you do in response? If your behaviors have changed, in response to the failure, how did they?

_____

_____

_____

_____

How did it feel to reflect on that moment? I had us do this reflection because reflection is key to growth. It helps us see ways we can adjust and alter when needed. The best type of reflection is planned reflection. Truth be told, we all reflect over things in some form of fashion; but it is not always productive.

This was a major key I acquired during my social work studies. In the field of interpersonal support and therapy it is imperative that you are able to be transparent with yourself. If we cannot be honest with ourselves, we have a long battle ahead. During reflection, we find peace in understanding what is really happening. Most times, failing at something doesn't technically mean you aren't supposed to do it. It could mean it isn't meant for right now, or there are some things you have to learn in order to be prepared.

That's what happened to me in 2015. It was during my time of working on my Masters of Social Work when I realized I wanted to impact community development and advocacy from the field of education. I realized it when looking at the three major pillars that affect the sustainability of a community; economics, politics, and education. Education is at the foundation of them all. Without a proper education, you are unable to be fiscally secure. Without proper education, you won't be knowledgeable or have the critical thinking needed to make informed decisions. It hit me that Education is the heart of community growth and development.

It was during this year that I began doing research on different alternative teacher preparation programs, because I was absolutely against going back to undergrad for more classes. I narrowed my search down to The New Teacher Project (TNTP) in Baltimore and Teach for America (TFA) with high hopes of the Memphis Region. The spring semester of my program rolled around and I began having interviews for both TNTP and TFA. After making it to the final round with both, I was offered a position with TNTP in Baltimore and was rejected by TFA.

It hit me at that moment, I received a loud resounding no from a program I wanted to be a part of. I was hurt.

I took this time to still look around for positions in the area because I wasn't completely sold on TNTP. The reality is, my first option was TFA and I felt I would make a great corps member. Soon after, I interviewed for a position in Milwaukee, WI. In the position, I would build a new community-based assistance program and serve as the first coordinator. So now, I had two positions to choose from. One in Baltimore, MD; a city I have always loved to visit. The other, in dreary Milwaukee.

The position in Baltimore would allow me to get into teaching and the opportunity in Milwaukee would give me more organizational development skills. Knowing in the back of my head that TFA was my first choice, I chose to go to Milwaukee and apply to TFA again. That is exactly what I did. I took what I learned from my first round of interviewing with TFA and applied it to this time around. I bought a book that teaches you how to maximize your application and strengths and I talked to people who had been a part of TFA.

It was around my birthday when I found out I had not only been accepted, but I was placed in Memphis, TN which was in my top 2 choices both application cycles. It was finally my time. I can't help but think about where I may be now if I had chosen to not apply again. I truly believe I joined TFA when I was supposed to. Great relationships were built with peers, and I had the chance to join a first-year charter school. I learned so much during my time with TFA.

There may be something that has kept you from pursuing a goal of yours. My greatest advice to you is to not let that stop you. I'd be a liar if I told you it was going to be a simple task, but it is not. There are some days when I feel overwhelmed with an issue and I may even cry. I don't fault myself for expressing my human side. The difference is that I do not give up. Neither should you. Even when you feel like you can't figure it out; keep going because there is success in failure.

In chapter three, I introduced the concept of what it means to L.I.V.E. as we are working towards our purpose and goals. To L.I.V.E. is to:
1. Live in your personal truth
2. Identify and reflect on past failures

3. Validate and find balance within your life
4. Erase Fear

There are so many moving pieces that go into pursuing something new and it is my hopes that we all walk in our individual purposes. Let's not allow our fear of failure and time to interfere in what is in our heart. Instead, go in with an open mind and watch everything come along beautifully.

Period.

If you didn't get anything else from this book, I hope you've come to terms with the fact that everything has a purpose. Each of our journeys toward purpose looks different, so celebrate the uniqueness of your story.

Let go and fly like a butterfly.

~Moe

Acknowledgements

Writing a book is no easy task; especially when you have your brain and heart strings pulled in every which way. From being a doctoral student, publishing consultant, nail polish creator, and educator, there is never a shortage of work for me to do. I'm actually thinking about petitioning for a few extra hours in the day. Ha!

I would like to take a moment to thank those individuals in my life who have been here with me throughout the process of juggling multiple roles. It has not always been easy managing it all, but it all gets done 100% at the end of the day. If it weren't for my village showing up for me when needed, I don't know where I'd be. Seriously!

I appreciate my mentors for continuously pushing me further throughout my professional career. I thank you for allowing me to not only see what is in front of me, but to see the potential I have within research and academia. It has been a long-held goal and dream of mine, and it feels surreal seeing it all unfold in front of my eyes.

I would like to thank my aunts, both blood and pseudo. You all have really been a keen heart both physically and spiritually. It has been extremely hard since my grandmother passed away and the transition was the hardest I've ever had to make. As shared within the book, although there are positive lessons found in sad moments, that doesn't mean you aren't allowed to feel the pain of them. I allow myself to feel because it keeps me pushing; because it reminds me that I am alive.

So, to my village, friends, and loved ones who have been a strong force of encouragement and support as I embark on yet another journey; I thank you. I would like to say thank you to my friends who have entrusted me with their secrets and innermost feelings in confidence. It was the strength you all displayed by telling your story that pushed me to continue in my purpose.

It was after the release of They Never Told when I really realized how many people had a story lying dormant inside them waiting to be shared. You all are my *why* and my motivation to continue. Because of you, I'm encouraged even more to motivate others to live out loud in their personal truths and journeys.

About the Author

Moe Nicole, MSW, M.Ed. is currently pursuing her Doctorate in Education from the University of Memphis. While a full-time student, she serves as an instructor for older adults with disabilities and as a full-time entrepreneur by providing publishing consulting services for new authors and creating nail polish for LOL Nail Lacquer. Moe's ultimate goal is to encourage and motivate other people to live within their personal truths and follow their goals and purpose, especially during the difficult times.

Let's stay connected!

Websites: www.MoeNicole.com
www.liveoutloudtoday.com
Facebook: www.facebook.com/moenicoleb
Instagram: @MoeNicoleB

Other Books by Moe Nicole

So, you want to write a book?

In this book, Moe outlines an overview of the self-publishing process for 1st time authors. The book is meant to be used as a guide to outline the various steps in the process.

They Never Told

They Never Told follows four adults who are survivors of childhood sexual assault. By connecting with each person, the reader is taken through important intrapersonal journeys and learn ways to build stronger relationships with the youth in their lives.

30 Things I learned about Love before my golden 30th Birthday

In this book, Moe shares the top lessons she has learned regarding love with various relationships in her life. She reflects on love from various perspectives, such as platonic, family, and relationships.

Made in United States
North Haven, CT
14 September 2024

57445377R00082